LESS OIL OR MORE CASKETS

LESS OIL OR MORE CASKETS

The National Security Argument for Moving Away from Oil

Gregory A. Ballard

Mayor of Indianapolis
2008–2015
Lt. Col., US Marine Corps (Ret.)
1978–2001

Indiana University Press

This book is a publication of

Indiana University Press
Office of Scholarly Publishing
Herman B Wells Library 350
1320 East 10th Street
Bloomington, Indiana 47405 USA

iupress.indiana.edu

Manufactured in the United States of America

ISBN 978-0-253-03744-2 (pbk.)
ISBN 978-0-253-03745-9 (web PDF)

1 2 3 4 5   23 22 21 20 19 18

This book is dedicated to all the members of the United States military who have fought and died over the last forty years, and to those who continue to fight, to ensure that the world has sufficient energy resources. May their numbers be far fewer in the future.

Contents

Acknowledgments

MY WIFE, WINNIE, has been with me over thirty-five years. She has been a stalwart by my side: through my Marine career, a war, my transition back into the civilian world, my eight years as a mayor, and now as we head into a more reflective period in our lives. If I've had any success, it is a result of her staying by my side.

The University of Indianapolis has been very supportive of my postmayoral efforts, including this book. Its president, Rob Manuel, and its former provost and now president of the Independent Colleges of Indiana, David Wantz, have helped tremendously, as have so many of the great staff.

My initial editor, Peter Noot, was tremendous in making the book more readable while keeping my voice. Jeannine Allen was very helpful in providing graphical and technical support on the manuscript. Dawn Pearson was instrumental with the photos in the book. As I learned, this can be very frustrating, but Dawn hung in there, and I am very appreciative. Carrie O'Connor, who was also my speechwriter while I was the mayor, provided some important initial comments.

Over the last few years, two organizations, Securing America's Future Energy and the Truman Project for National Security, helped shape and hone my views on this important, emerging topic. In particular, Victoria Gurevich of the Truman Project went well beyond what I was expecting when I asked her a few questions. Additionally, Roger Sorkin, who created the powerful documentary, *The Burden*, provided focus to my views. Kellie Walsh, along with Graham Richard, formerly of Advanced Energy Economy, have also been very supportive in this regard.

Melissa Proffitt Schmidt and Holly Banta have been critical in ensuring everything surrounding the book was done correctly. I'm always astounded at all the legal and administrative requirements in writing a book.

Indiana University Press, particularly Ashley Runyon, was stellar in its support of this effort. I was always amazed at how quickly and professionally they responded to my questions. I can't thank them enough.

Lastly, I would like to thank all those who helped me in my Marine career. It was a true honor to serve my country for twenty-three years in uniform, and that service developed me in so many ways that continue to positively affect my life still today. Words cannot adequately express my gratitude.

Moving Away from Oil: Why Now?

Today, when we send our young men and women off to war, we pat them on the back and thank them for their service. We throw parades and homecomings upon their successful return. We sadly salute the caskets as they go by. Then we drive down to the neighborhood gas station and fill up—and nobody makes the connection; no one sees the irony.

The simple question must be asked: Why are we in the Middle East? Why do we continue to pour enormous resources into an area of the world that has cost us so dearly, in both human and financial terms, over the last forty years?

We do this to maintain the global oil market. Historically, that market has been crucial to the Western standard of living because the world relied on oil for its numerous energy requirements. But that has changed. Today, the use of oil most relevant to our quality of life is for transportation energy—how we move people and goods.

Transportation is the last industry dominated by the use of oil. Electric power generated by oil is virtually nonexistent, and uses for oil in residential and commercial heating continue to fall. Only transportation and industrial uses consume significant quantities of oil in the United States, and transportation is by far the dominant user—over 70 percent of total oil consumption, according to the Energy Information Administration. Worldwide, the percentage of oil consumption for transport has risen from 45 percent in 1973 to 64 percent in 2012, according to the International Energy Agency. Oil still is used for over 90 percent of transportation needs in our country and the world, and it will remain so unless new technology is understood and embraced.

Transportation energy technology is on the cusp of great changes that will allow the international economy to be free of oil's chokehold. The technology of the past mandated that the United States devote enormous resources to preserving the flow of oil, not just to the United States but to all markets, so as to maintain global demand for goods and services, preserving the international economy. But emerging technologies allow us to change that dynamic. This technology will not cause us to lose our standard of living; indeed, it may enhance it. It will, however, change the strategic dynamic wherein the United States must defend—at enormous cost—the flow of oil, which allows the world to send money to people who want to kill us. Today, we are funding both sides of the War on Terror.

In a teaser for Roger Sorkin's 2015 documentary *The Burden* (I appear in the film), a former soldier says, "In a three-month span, I buried two guys. When I squeeze the gas pump, you know, I think about it. . . . Why should their families have to bear that burden?" SAFE (Securing America's Future Energy), a non-partisan nonprofit dedicated to ending our dependence on oil, has more than a dozen retired four-star generals and admirals on its board. The military understands this issue. The Pentagon knows the importance of moving away from oil.

Talk of "supporting the troops" seems to fall on deaf ears, politically, whenever reducing our dependence on oil is mentioned. Supporting the troops can take on many dimensions, but sending them into conflict *only when necessary* should be a primary tenet. Improving conditions for the future, so that troops would not be needed, would seem to follow. Foreseeing the future is critical.

When I went to the Gulf War in 1990–91, maintaining the global flow of oil was critical to our quality of life. At that point, our level of technology could not overcome our need for the resources in the Middle East. There is no question that a disruption to the flow of oil at that time would have severely, if not catastrophically, affected the global economy.

The following remarks confirm this:

- Former Secretary of State James Baker told PBS's *Frontline* that the vital national interest was to "secure access to the energy resources of the Persian Gulf."
- On March 17, 2005, Senator Richard Lugar put into the Congressional Record: "The underlying goal of the U.N. force, which included 500,000 American troops, was to ensure continued and unfettered access to petroleum."

Since then, our actions as a nation have been largely to address the supply side of the economic equation. Fracking, the Keystone Pipeline, and other efforts are caught up in politics but don't actually address reality. That reality is that, according to a 2017 CNN.com report, OPEC has 81 percent of the known oil reserves, and the United States is not in the top 10 countries for reserves; that China, India, and other growing nations will continue to buy that OPEC oil unless new technology is adopted; and that, as a result, terrorism will continue to be funded. It is a fool's errand to continuously address supply when reducing demand is the real key to minimizing the influence of the Middle East and bringing our troops home. And we can dramatically reduce demand over the next ten to twenty years.

It's time to move away from oil as the primary transportation fuel. Because of our current transportation model, the world continues to fight wars, manage conflicts, lose thousands of lives, and spend enormous financial resources. We have been doing so for over forty years.

All of that cost has been simply to maintain the flow of oil throughout the world. It's time to admit that. It's also time to change.

LESS OIL or MORE CASKETS

1 What Is the Situation?

OIL HAS BEEN used as a weapon against the United States for decades. The oil embargoes of the 1970s told the world that the quality of life and standard of living of oil-dependent nations are beholden to Middle Eastern oil. Since then, well-funded terrorism has been the result. Here are three examples:

- Iran, which detained fifty-two United States hostages for 444 days from 1979 to 1981, and has been designated by the State Department as a "State Sponsor of Terrorism" since 1984, derives about 60 percent of its revenue from oil. That number will only increase now that sanctions have been lifted and Iran has negotiated with China for oil.
- Al-Qaeda was well funded by a complex network of donations from wealthy businessmen and diverted charity donations. Oil was the original source of that wealth. We all know of the havoc that Osama bin Laden wreaked on the world before his death. The deaths and financial resources expended to counter al-Qaeda were enormous.
- ISIS, according to leading publications, depends on the sale of oil on the black market for a large portion of its revenue. Some estimates are that ISIS oil revenue accounts for over half of the organization's income. That was definitely true in the formative stages, but ISIS has diversified revenues since 2015. However, oil is still a major source of its income, and there are estimates that ISIS had at one time in excess of $2 billion in cash. According to Andreas Krieg, a military scholar at King's College London in Qatar, "the Islamic State is certainly the best financially endowed terrorist organization in history."[1]

When you combine the fact that terrorism is still funded largely by oil revenues with the fact that 70 percent of oil is used for transportation, it does not seem overly complicated to surmise that reducing demand is critical. We could not do that before. But now we can.

Too many people believe that increasing supply is the answer. That is wrong. It looks and feels good in the short term, but it is not the answer. Reducing demand is the answer because there is no free market for oil. It is important to understand that about 80 percent of the known oil reserves in the world are in the hands of national oil companies—effectively in the hands of national leaders. These are not commercial entities subject to normal market forces. As we have seen throughout the last few decades, the world's supply of oil is controlled by countries whose interests are not aligned with ours. They will open or close the spigot, raising or lowering the price of oil, to their advantage, not to ours.

Also, the United States will remain committed to preserving the flow of oil throughout the world in order to protect international trade and our own economy. If most countries we trade with did not require oil for their transportation needs, we would not have to spend the enormous resources we do now to maintain that flow of oil (estimated by *The Burden* to be $85 billion annually).

The only way to reduce the enormous resources being spent to protect the flow of oil is to change our transportation technology, thereby dramatically reducing demand. Then we could start to bring our troops home and reduce funding for terrorism.

The sad part of all of this is that it has been going on for decades. Our nation haltingly moves in the right direction at times, but the efforts have been largely talk. What our leaders have been saying and what actually happens are two different tales.

In reality, we have done very little.

Rhetoric vs. Action

I have great respect for the office of the president, but it's illuminating to look at the contrast between rhetoric and national action over the years. Not all blame is resident in only one office, and Congress can easily block action, but the words below reflect what our nation has been saying and doing over the past forty years.

Here is a sampling of presidential quotations all the way back to 1973 as excerpted from an October 31, 2008, Associated Press article in the *San Diego Union-Tribune* (except for the last George W. Bush quote, which is from a State of the Union address). Reading these quotations together, one could easily come to the conclusion that officeholders at the national level address energy merely as a talking point to assuage current situations or gain political favor with the public, rather than as an effort to solve the problem. Keeping troops in the Middle East is the result.

Read the quotations first. Then note the summary of what actually happened during the terms of these presidents.

What the Presidents Said

Richard Nixon, responding to the Arab oil embargo, November 7, 1973:

> *Let us set our national goal . . . that by the end of this decade we will have developed the potential to meet our own energy needs without depending on any foreign energy sources. Let us pledge that by 1980, under Project Independence, we shall be able to meet America's energy needs from America's own energy resources.*

Gerald Ford, State of the Union address, January 15, 1975:

> *I am recommending a plan to make us invulnerable to cutoffs of foreign oil. It will require sacrifice, but it—and this is most important—it will work.*

Jimmy Carter, in a television address on July 15, 1979, in which he announced temporary oil import quotas:

> *This intolerable dependence on foreign oil threatens our economic independence and the very security of our nation. . . . Beginning this moment, this nation will never use more foreign oil than we did in 1977—never.*

Ronald Reagan, in an energy security message to Congress on May 6, 1987, in which he raised concerns about "our increasing dependence on imported oil":

> *We must take steps to better protect ourselves from potential oil supply interruptions and increase our energy and national security.*

George H. W. Bush, in an address to Congress on September 11, 1990, in the run-up to the Gulf War:

> *Conservation efforts are essential to keep our energy needs as low as possible. And we must take advantage of our energy sources across the board: coal, natural gas, hydro, and nuclear. Our failure to do these things has made us more dependent on foreign oil than ever before.*

Bill Clinton, in an energy security statement on February 16, 1995:

> *The nation's growing reliance on imports of crude oil and refined products threatens the nation's security because they make us more vulnerable to oil supply disruptions.*

George W. Bush, State of the Union address, February 7, 2001:

> *We can promote alternative energy sources and conservation, and we must. America must become more energy independent, and we will.*

George W. Bush, State of the Union, 2006:

> *We have a serious problem. America is addicted to oil, which is often imported from unstable parts of the world.*

What Actually Happened

The words:

Richard Nixon, responding to the Arab oil embargo, November 7, 1973:

> **Let us set our national goal . . . that by the end of this decade we will have developed the potential to meet our own energy needs without depending**

> *on any foreign energy sources. Let us pledge that by 1980, under Project Independence, we shall be able to meet America's energy needs from America's own energy resources.*

The reality:

When Britain withdrew from the Persian Gulf in the late 1960s/early 1970s, the United States had mounting Cold War tensions with the Soviet Union, including the Vietnam War. To preclude Soviet action in the Middle East while trying not to become engaged directly, President Nixon created the "Twin Pillars Strategy," which tried to establish Iran and Saudi Arabia as regional powers. They were encouraged to acquire copious amounts of advanced arms from the US government to support their new roles as "regional policemen."

Soon thereafter Iran and Saudi Arabia were a major part of the 1973–74 oil embargo by OPEC (Organization of the Petroleum Exporting Countries) in response to the 1973 Yom Kippur War. Oil prices tripled. Price controls were instituted to pacify the public but—as price controls almost always do—contributed to the artificial shortage and resulted in people standing in line for hours to get gasoline for their cars.

None of this spurred positive action for the nation. The percentage of imports in the early 1970s was around 30 percent and would rise to over 40 percent in the 1980s. OPEC now realized the enormous leverage they had over the West, and arming Iran and Saudi Arabia ushered in a pattern of Middle Eastern militarism that contributed to the destabilization of the region that continues to this day.

The words:

Gerald Ford, State of the Union address January 15, 1975:

> *I am recommending a plan to make us invulnerable to cutoffs of foreign oil. It will require sacrifice, but it—and this is most important—it will work.*

The reality:

President Ford was focused on achieving energy independence and proposed to Congress what he called the "first comprehensive national energy program." Congress passed legislation intended to phase out the price controls on domestic oil and focused on increasing the supply of oil. This legislation also created the Strategic Petroleum Reserve. President Ford instituted a voluntary automobile efficiency program to increase gasoline mileage; this was believed to be the first time that such a program had been instituted at the national level.

Although he was president for only two and a half years, President Ford was active in trying to improve the energy situation in America, given the level of available technology and a Congress that was not always on board with his direction. Meanwhile, the percentage of oil imports continued upward.

The words:

Jimmy Carter, in a television address on July 15, 1979, in which he announced temporary oil import quotas:

> *This intolerable dependence on foreign oil threatens our economic independence and the very security of our nation. . . . Beginning this moment, this nation will never use more foreign oil than we did in 1977—never.*

The reality:

The words are strong. President Carter believed that oil was a limited resource and that we must move away from it before it runs out. Conservation was his emphasis. He found little support for this train of thought, which included a tax on oil. Then the Iranian Revolution of 1979 (when American hostages were held for 444 days) decreased the global supply, and prices went up again. Long lines returned to the gas pumps.

After that, the world situation changed. In response to the Soviet Union's December 1979 invasion of Afghanistan, President Carter, in his State of the Union Address in January 1980 (after the strong words above), stated that the United States would use military force if necessary to defend its national interests in the Persian Gulf. He stated that Soviet troops in Afghanistan posed

> a grave threat to the free movement of Middle East oil. . . . Meeting this challenge will take national will, diplomatic and political wisdom, economic sacrifice, and, of course, military capability. We must call on the best that is in us to preserve the security of this crucial region. Let our position be absolutely clear: An attempt by any outside force to gain control of the Persian Gulf region will be regarded as an assault on the vital interests of the United States of America, and such an assault will be repelled by any means necessary, including military force.

A buildup of military forces in the Middle East ensued. So much for conservation. Meanwhile, the percentage of oil imports continued upward.

Also, very early in President Carter's term, the Department of Energy was created. It began on October 1, 1977, and it consolidated the Federal Energy Administration, the Energy Research and Development Administration, the Federal Power Commission, and programs of various other agencies.

From July 1970 to July 1980, oil prices rose from $3.31 per barrel to $39.50 per barrel, more than a tenfold increase, largely as the result of OPEC actions.

Of historical note, the Synthetic Fuels Corporation was established in 1980 by the federal government in response to the second major oil disruption in less than a decade. Although the move to encourage the development of synthetic fuel manufacturing was well intended, 1980s market forces concerning oil doomed this effort.

Of more long-term importance, Deng Xiaoping assumed control in China in 1978. He instituted widespread economic reforms and opened China to the global economy, which included foreign investment. As a result, after Mao Zedong's death, China became one of the fastest-growing economies in the world, moving hundreds of millions of Chinese into the middle class. Over the last forty years, the number of cars in China has grown from almost none to more than 150 million today. China is now the largest producer and seller of vehicles in the world, which also means that the nation is a large consumer and importer of oil—it now moves that market. Thus, perhaps the least-talked-about but still dangerous foreign policy issue today is the relationship between China and Iran.

The words:
Ronald Reagan, in an energy security message to Congress on May 6, 1987, in which he raised concerns about "our increasing dependence on imported oil":

> *We must take steps to better protect ourselves from potential oil supply interruptions and increase our energy and national security.*

The reality:
President Reagan dismantled much of the Carter-era economics, including energy policy, but he continued to increase American participation in the Middle East, an area that still relies heavily on oil for its economic health. Reagan's two terms largely coincided with the eight-year Iran-Iraq War, wherein the United States, in an attempt to maintain stability in the region, largely supported Iraq's brutal dictator, Saddam Hussein. Both countries are traditionally heavy oil exporters. To fill the oil supply gap, Saudi Arabia kept production at such a level as to preclude a dramatic increase in prices.

Also, the bombing of a US Marine compound in Beirut, Lebanon, killed 241 troops. Again, an attempt to maintain stability in the region resulted in tragedy for the United States. President Reagan extracted all troops from Beirut a few months later.

President Reagan and his advisers believed in a free market and fewer regulations. He largely eliminated all government intervention into the market, including controls on the production and distribution of oil. In 1980, the price of oil was around $40 per barrel but fell into the teens just a few years afterward and remained largely stable until the 2000s. The price of gasoline at the pump also came down. Supply problems vanished. Since transportation technology was essentially unchanged, there was movement away from the more-gas-efficient cars developed during the 1970s to less-efficient cars.

To be fair, there were some internal dynamics within OPEC that helped global oil prices stay down. But removing government controls within the United States helped. Reliance on foreign oil did decrease during President Reagan's two terms, but perhaps more importantly, the sources of that foreign oil started to come from friendlier nations like Canada and Mexico rather than OPEC.

The words:

George H. W. Bush, in an address to Congress on September 11, 1990, in the run-up to the Gulf War:

> *Conservation efforts are essential to keep our energy needs as low as possible. And we must take advantage of our energy sources across the board: coal, natural gas, hydro, and nuclear. Our failure to do these things has made us more dependent on foreign oil than ever before.*

The reality:

In August 1990, fresh from fighting Iran for eight years, Iraq invaded the neighboring country of Kuwait, claiming some of Kuwait's oil-rich lands as its own. Although some countries contended the Iraqi buildup toward Kuwait was a bluff, Saddam Hussein sent one hundred forty thousand troops into Kuwait, capturing the country very quickly. By doing so, Saddam Hussein gained control over a much larger amount of the world's oil supply, which could damage the oil-dependent economies of Western nations, along with others.

In its first major test after the end of the Cold War (the Berlin Wall had fallen in 1989), America and its more than two dozen allies—which, encouragingly, included several Arab nations—deployed over half a million troops. I was one of them. With the backing of the United Nations, with China and Russia on the sidelines, and with Israel being convinced to sit out so that Arab nations could join the coalition, the impressive multinational force pushed Iraq back across its borders in less than two months of full-scale operations.

The rhetoric surrounding the rationale for expelling Iraq from Kuwait is illuminating, and is similar to how we talk about oil and war today. In his address to the nation on January 16, 1991, just after the air operations portion of the war began, President Bush talked of a "new world order" and the "liberation of Kuwait." The word "oil" was never mentioned. Others at the time talked about "countering aggression" and "expelling a dictator."

This entire war was about maintaining the free flow of oil around the world, but no one in an official capacity was willing to say so.

Once again, here are the words of former Secretary of State James Baker and former Senator Richard Lugar, *after* the war:

> BAKER: The vital national interest was to "secure access to the energy resources of the Persian Gulf."
>
> LUGAR: "The underlying goal of the U.N. force, which included 500,000 American troops, was to ensure continued and unfettered access to petroleum."

I had no problem whatsoever with the Gulf War. It was needed to maintain the global economic order. In my mind, there is no question about that. I was proud to serve. However, the perspective afforded by looking back decades later is important.

By far the hardest day of my twenty-three-year Marine career was the day I left for the Gulf War. I was the operations officer for my battalion and was part of its advance party that deployed in December 1990. My wife drove me to our staging area, and because I was the officer in charge of the movement, she had to leave almost immediately after we arrived so that I could attend to my duties. We had two very young children at that time. The press was estimating that there would be tens of thousands of casualties in the first few days of the war, due to the large number of forces involved and the potential for the use of chemical weapons. To this day, I remember the look on my wife's face as I turned away to prepare for deployment. It was beyond description. I want fewer troops and families to experience such pain.

In retrospect, that my nation could send all of us to war without honestly admitting to the public why we were necessary is hurtful. What is much more painful, however, is that we continue to expend lives and other resources to maintain this flow of oil around the world, knowing that it feeds our enemies. How we can continue to refuse to acknowledge this fact is baffling. Admitting this reality would be a good first step.

Again, why are we in the Middle East?

The words:

Bill Clinton, in an energy security statement on February 16, 1995:

> *The nation's growing reliance on imports of crude oil and refined products threatens the nation's security because they make us more vulnerable to oil supply disruptions.*

The reality:

Unfortunately for President Clinton, Osama bin Laden shifted his focus from Russia to the United States, at least partially as a result of US action in the 1990–91 Gulf War. Although President Clinton conducted some military actions against Iraq and levied oil sanctions against Iran in 1995, he spent much of his two terms experiencing terrorism at the hands of bin Laden and his organization, al-Qaeda. Terrorist actions during his two terms included:

- The World Trade Center bombing, New York City, 1993
- The bombing of the Saudi military installation, Riyadh, 1995
- The bombing of Khobar Towers, Dhahran, 1996
- The East Africa Embassy bombings, 1998
- The bombing of the USS *Cole*, Aden, Yemen, 2000

Americans died in every one of these incidents. (More information about specific terrorist incidents is detailed in a later chapter.) What is significant about these bombings, but is almost never talked about, is how al-Qaeda was funded. The next chapter, which highlights two War College papers written in the early

2000s, explains much about the funding mechanisms for al-Qaeda. Oil money was the centerpiece.

Still, oil imports topped 50 percent during President Clinton's term.

The words:

George W. Bush, State of the Union address, February 7, 2001:

We can promote alternative energy sources and conservation, and we must. America must become more energy independent, and we will.

George W. Bush, State of the Union, 2006:

We have a serious problem. America is addicted to oil, which is often imported from unstable parts of the world.

The reality:

After the September 11 attacks, President Bush's two terms were focused primarily on national security, as they should have been. He has mentioned frequently how much that conversation dominated his presidency. Certainly, most Americans who lived through that tragic day understand.

Wars in Iraq and Afghanistan began in retaliation, which took enormous resources, both in lives and money. However, a backdrop to the immediate need for security was the continuing need to ensure the flow of oil around the world while fighting in the Middle East.

Based on his actions after 9/11 and his statement above regarding America's oil addiction, in which he said that oil is often imported from unstable parts of the world, President Bush clearly saw energy as a national security issue. During a 2000 presidential debate with Al Gore, Bush said, "Today we import a million barrels from Saddam Hussein. I would rather that a million come from our own hemisphere, our own country, as opposed [to] from Saddam Hussein."

These are good sentiments. I certainly agree that energy is first and foremost a national security issue, but even today, if America imported no oil from the Middle East, it would matter little to world security. Nations in Asia and other parts of the world outside America send hundreds of billions of dollars to the Middle East in exchange for oil. The funding of terrorism will continue until we address that phenomenon. Only changing transportation technology globally will allow this change.

Hybrid technology in vehicles was starting to catch on in this era, particularly with the then-revolutionary car, the Toyota Prius. However, oil dependence would reach 60 percent during the 2000s.

In retrospect, these presidents' remarks about reducing or eliminating our need for foreign oil are baffling. After many of these statements, the United States did essentially nothing. Despite the oil embargo in the early 1970s, reliance on foreign oil continued to increase: from 28 percent in the early 1970s to over 40 percent in the mid-1980s, eventually surpassing 60 percent reliance on foreign oil in the 2000s before finally pulling back.

Implicit in almost all of the presidential statements above is the suggestion that oil is a national commodity rather than a global one. That is completely wrong. The United States cannot control the global oil market. Unfortunately, the public has been misinformed about this for decades.

We have had, and continue to have, little to no influence over the price of a barrel of oil. During the embargo in the early 1970s, oil prices tripled. Still today, the fluctuation of the price of oil is largely dependent on whether the spigot is turned on or off by OPEC. (See Appendix B to view the price fluctuation of a barrel of oil from 1986 to 2015.)

There has been some minimal improvement lately. According to the Energy Information Administration, in 2015, only 24 percent of the petroleum consumed by the United States is imported, while the leading oil exporter to the United States was Canada, whose oil importation is of no concern whatsoever. However, Saudi Arabia and Venezuela are in the top five countries exporting to the United States, and that is a bit problematic. Far more problematic are the large and growing economies around the world, such as China and India, with which we conduct trade, while they buy oil from countries involved in terrorism.

Energy Independence Is Nice, But Irrelevant

According to our presidents and almost everyone else, energy independence is paramount. For years I have disagreed with this sentiment. Energy independence is something that almost all federal officeholders talk about, including all of our presidents and most presidential candidates. But I would contend that while our energy independence may be a nice step, it is hardly meaningful in the overall picture. It may make for effective political campaign rhetoric, but the reality is something else.

As shown in figure 1.1 (from multiple sources), even before the recent sanctions, Iran was largely exporting to Europe and Asia. After the sanctions, China, India, Japan, and South Korea were the top four destinations for Iranian oil. How is American energy independence going to affect oil dollars flowing into this US-designated state sponsor of terrorism? Not at all. Also, as seen in figure 1.2, Saudi Arabia ships most of its oil to Asia.

As long as China, India, and other nations around the world continue to increase their use of oil at the level they have in recent years, our energy independence barely moves the needle in reducing the need for this global commodity. Even if we somehow used only our own resources for transportation, it would not matter, because the energy required for transportation worldwide would still be propping up an oil market that allows the Middle East to export hundreds of

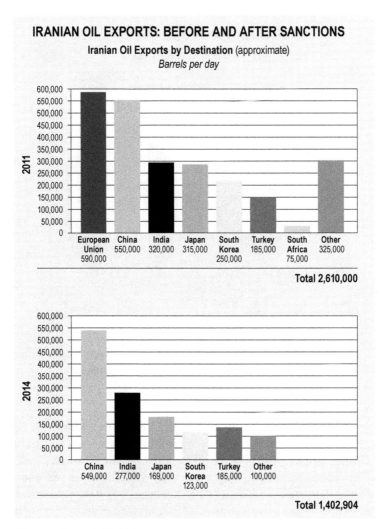

Figure 1.1. Sources: Multiple

billions of dollars' worth of oil every year—much of which turns into money for terrorists. Some estimates are that half a trillion dollars annually is sent to the Middle East to buy oil by countries other than the United States. That transfer of wealth funds our enemies. Also, it is the United States that continues to spend money to protect the oil infrastructure to ensure this flow of oil to those markets with which we continue to trade. As we do that, enormous sums of money continue to flow to our adversaries. This seems obvious, but almost no one ever talks about it.

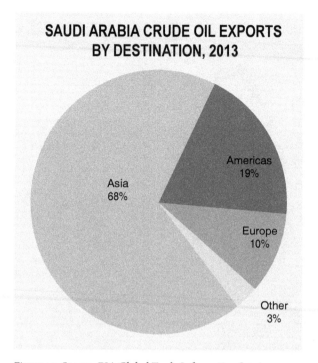

Figure 1.2. Source: EIA Global Trade Information Services

The Global Oil Chokepoints map that follows is well known to military and national security experts (source: Energy Information Administration). It shows the importance of the flow of oil from the Middle East to the rest of the world. The United States spends approximately $70 billion per year protecting chokepoints—bottlenecks where a disruption could be catastrophic if a flow of material stopped—and other infrastructure from pirates and other threats, so that oil can flow both to the United States and to our trading partners. (I've seen estimates from $67 billion to $300 billion, but I believe that $70 billion is the generally recognized figure.)

This is above and beyond the costs for the wars and conflicts we have fought over the last few decades in the Middle East. At great cost, the United States is subsidizing both the producers and consumers of the oil that flows through these chokepoints. We will continue to do this so that global trade can continue.

Putting the Puzzle Together

Many people see snippets of information, but rarely do they see how all of this information tells the story. A number of charts and other information help to

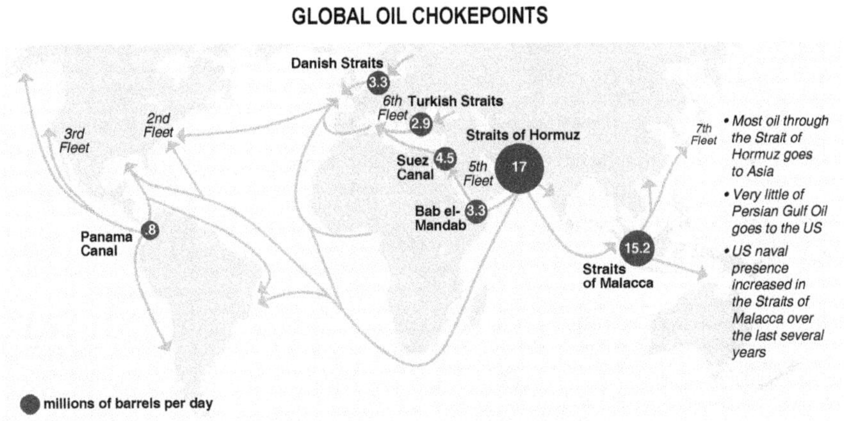

GLOBAL OIL CHOKEPOINTS

Map 1.1.

explain where we are now and the possible implications for increased reliance on oil for the world's transportation needs. Let's put the puzzle together.

How Much Oil Is Produced Each Year, and Who Is Producing It?

The data in table 1.1 provide information about oil production in selective years and are indicative of the larger trend that has resulted in the costs that are described in a subsequent chapter. Percentages are based on overall world production (rounded off). This data comes from the Energy Information Administration and is listed in the *Transportation Energy Data Book*. Production more or less mirrors consumption as producers respond to the market.

In 1960, the year that OPEC was formed, the United States produced 7 million barrels of crude oil per day, which was just over 33 percent of the world total of 20.99 million barrels per day. OPEC, which then consisted of just five countries (Iraq, Iran, Kuwait, Saudi Arabia, and Venezuela), produced about 41 percent of crude oil, just under 9 million barrels per day.

The United States has not produced anywhere near 33 percent of the world's crude oil in decades. In the troubled times of the 1970s, US crude production largely remained near 15 percent, and from 2006 to 2008, production fell below 7 percent for three consecutive years. In 2014, US production nudged over 10 percent for the first time since 1996.

Meanwhile, OPEC produced over 50 percent of the world's crude oil for many years in the 1970s and produced at least 40 percent every year that decade. The lowest percentage produced since 1960 was 28.5 percent in 1985, but since 1993, OPEC has produced over 40 percent of the world's crude oil every year, with the exception of 2002 (39.3 percent). That outsized influence has had enormous consequences.

Table 1.1: World Crude Oil Production (in millions of barrels per day)

Year	United States	OPEC	World (total)
1960	7.04 (33%)	8.70 (41%)	20.99
1970	9.64 (21%)	23.30 (51%)	45.89
1973*	9.21 (16%)	29.66 (53%)	55.68
1980	8.60 (14%)	25.38 (43%)	59.56
1990	7.36 (12%)	22.50 (37%)	60.50
2000	5.82 (8%)	28.94 (42%)	68.53
2010	5.48 (7%)	32.00 (43%)	74.65
2014	8.65 (11%)	32.43 (42%)	77.83

* Year of oil embargoes

Table 1.2: United States Share of World Petroleum Consumption (selected years)

Year	Percentage
1960	46%
1970	31%
1980	27%
1990	25%
2000	26%
2010	22%

The United States' Share of Consumption

The United States' share of worldwide consumption continues to fall, as table 1.2 shows (source: Energy Information Administration). However, this is more reflective of the growth of other countries than of a reduced dependence on oil in the United States.

Who Has the Oil Reserves?

As you can see in table 1.3, again using the Energy Information Administration's numbers, OPEC has the most reserves by a wide margin, indicating that they will be the dominant supplier of oil well into the future. Because OPEC continues to possess most of the known oil reserves—over 80 percent, according to a CNN report in 2017—the future does not look much different from the past few decades.

What Is the Global Trend in Transportation?

The number of vehicles per capita by country or area can predict future oil needs. (See table 1.4.) The trend is very clear. The worldwide demand for oil will continue

Table 1.3: World Oil Reserves (in billions of barrels)

Year	United States	OPEC	Rest of World
1980	31 (5%)	427 (66%)	185 (29%)
1993	25 (2%)	767 (77%)	205 (21%)
2013	33 (2%)	1205 (73%)	411 (25%)

Table 1.4: Vehicles per 1,000 people

Country/Region	2003	2013
United States	816.1	808.6
China	18.7	88.6
India	10.1	26.6
Brazil	114.8	197.5
Africa	22.6	34.6
Asia, Far East	45.0	81.9
Asia, Middle East	85.5	129.5
Canada	580.0	646.1
Central/South America	114.2	184.6
Europe, East	224.5	332.4
Europe, West	565.7	589.6
Indonesia	28.1	77.2

Source: Department of Energy

to increase, caused largely by growing economies such as those of China, India, and Brazil, which use an increasing number of automobiles. (Remember that the worldwide use of oil for transport has increased from 45 percent in 1973 to 64 percent in 2012.) Since oil is by far the primary fuel for transportation, OPEC, sitting on top of most of the known oil reserves in the world, has tremendous influence over the increasing standard of living throughout these countries.

It also means that, as long as cars are powered by internal combustion engines, the United States will continue to protect the world's oil infrastructure—at great cost—to permit trade.

We Do Have Leverage

Table 1.5 details just how important the oil sector is to many nations' fiscal solvency; these are estimated figures derived from the CIA *World Factbook*, a report from the International Monetary Fund, and a University of Pennsylvania, Penn Wharton Public Policy article, "The Political Economy of Oil in the Middle East."

Since oil is now primarily used for transportation, it is obvious that a dramatic change in how we fuel cars around the world would dramatically affect

Table 1.5: Percent of Government Revenue Derived from
the Oil Sector

Iran	60%
Iraq	90%
Kuwait	90%
Oman	70%
Qatar	70%
Saudi Arabia	80%

Table 1.6: Fiscal Break-even Price in Dollars per Barrel

Country	2014	2015	2016
Iran	128	104	84
Iraq	97	113	95
Saudi Arabia	82	91	100
Venezuela	138	160	180
Libya	140	180	190

the economies of the Middle East. Funding for terrorism could be virtually curtailed. The strategic leverage would shift to the now oil-dependent countries. The costs of protecting the oil market, both human and financial, would lessen precipitously.

Additionally, many Middle Eastern countries need the cost of a barrel of oil to remain above a certain price in order to maintain their social spending. A SAFE chart sourced by Roubini Global Economics (table 1.6) shows how much a barrel of oil must cost in the global market in order to maintain a country's economy—particularly its social spending. (Appendix C, "Even the Saudis Know," reveals how one Middle East country understands this completely.)

Isn't that interesting? As the percentage of government revenue derived from oil exports shows, the Middle Eastern countries are very dependent on large, emerging economies such as China and India using automobiles with internal combustion engines. Over the last few years, many OPEC countries have been dipping into their financial reserves to keep their economies, particularly social spending, at acceptable levels. When the price of a barrel of oil remains low (for instance, below $50 a barrel), countries with economies largely based on oil exports suffer greatly. Even better, if we move away from oil as a transportation fuel, those numbers escalate dramatically, putting great economic pressure on these countries. The oil-exporting countries would have to continue to dip into their financial reserves in order to maintain stability. That would shift strategic leverage around the world.

Until the new transportation technology becomes commonplace (led by the United States, I hope), China, India, and other growing economies will continue to import oil from those nations that seek to harm the United States and its allies. China in particular is solidifying relations with countries that have been funding our adversaries. China is the top buyer of Iranian oil, and Iran now has agreements with China for oil drilling.

Only a shift in our transportation energy can change the outsized influence of those countries that want to continue to do us harm. Again, how much does our energy independence matter if the rest of the world continues to send hundreds of billions of dollars annually to our enemies? The only way to lessen the burden of sending our troops into the Middle East is to dramatically reduce the demand for oil worldwide so that it is no longer necessary to defend the global oil infrastructure. If we begin soon, this can be done over the next ten to twenty years by changing the majority of transportation energy requirements from oil to other energy sources.

In other words, cut off the supply of money to the Middle East. Then our troops can come home.

Note

1. Jose Pagliery, "Inside the $2 Billion ISIS War Machine," *CNN Money*, December 6, 2015, https://money.cnn.com/2015/12/06/news/isis-funding/index.html.

2 A Short Military Analysis

As I have said, the military understands this situation completely. Because they fight our battles, all military branches continuously analyze future battlefield needs. This is much of the subject matter in Roger Sorkin's documentary *The Burden*. Ironically, a large quantity of fuel is used just to move fuel around the battlefield, and seeing how this is done is illuminating. Also, oil-based fuel powers generators, which have become ever more critical to maintaining proper temperature and conditions for the technology used today in combat. This is a major logistical burden.

Also, at the upper levels in the military, a continuing dialogue occurs as to the causes of conflict and how to prevent them. Some of the most strategic thinkers in our nation are at the senior levels in the military, and although too professional to comment, they continually must deal with political divisions in Washington that not only hamper our military's ability to carry out the mission but also, sadly, result in deaths that could have been avoided.

I was in the Gulf War of 1990–91, and I, along with everyone else at that time, understood the need to defend the oil market to maintain the global economy. However, the situation is different today. We can start moving away from oil as a transportation fuel. Increasingly, the military understands that our pattern of actions in the Middle East, in the long term, is of little consequence. We are still there in significant numbers, as we have been for four decades. There are short-term wins that are celebrated by politicians and occasionally by the public, but the fact is, we are still there.

A Military Planning Primer

Here is an introduction to military logic—using laymen's terms to avoid becoming overly technical or mired in jargon—that I hope will bring some light to the subject. Particularly enlightening is the work done by two War College students, Lt. Col. James Reilly and Lt. Col. Stephen Davis, over a decade ago. What they said then still applies today.

The Three Levels of War

There are three levels of war: strategic, operational, and tactical. The strategic level relates to the overall national aims. The operational level refers largely to the theater of operations, such as Europe or the Middle East. The tactical level generally concerns the fighting units, which directly engage an enemy.

An equivalent in the business world would be a large corporation, wherein the head offices formulate the overall strategy, the regional managers translate that strategy into policy and analyze how it applies to their region, and the workers at the lower levels actually implement the policy. As almost any experienced businessperson could tell you, the people at the various levels frequently see the strategy differently, and execution at the worker level can suffer.

Within the national security apparatus and the military, there are organizations that focus on the particular aims of each level. For instance, the White House/National Security Council would execute the strategic level. Today, the operational level would be run by what is called a Geographic Command, such as the US Central Command (which largely monitors the Middle East) or the US European Command. The tactical level would be the actual warfighters on the ground, in the air, and on the sea.

Ideally, the missions of the strategic, operational, and tactical levels are completely in sync and are executed accordingly. However, any reading of the history of war would suggest otherwise. Frequently, the operational and tactical levels see a completely different picture than the strategic thinkers do, and that mismatch can lead to tragedy or an unnecessarily prolonged struggle (e.g., Somalia and Vietnam). It is historically accurate to say that if the strategic-level goals and intentions are off the mark, then winning is impossible.

Center of Gravity

At each of these levels, commanders are taught to analyze the "center of gravity"— that is, both the enemy center of gravity and the friendly center of gravity. The term is attributed to the Prussian Carl von Clausewitz and appears in his renowned work *On War*, published posthumously in 1832 and still widely read and studied by military scholars today. The book is a difficult read but has many instances of great clarity. It is perhaps most famous for this quote: "War is merely the continuation of policy by other means."

Hundreds of scholarly papers have been written through the years about what Clausewitz meant by a "center of gravity," but his original definition of the "hub of all power and movement" is largely intact today. The exact quotation is: "One must keep the dominant characteristics of both belligerents in mind. Out of these characteristics a certain center of gravity develops, the hub of all power and movement, on which everything depends. That is the point against which all our energies should be directed." In 2008 the *Department of Defense Dictionary* defined the center of gravity as "the source of power that provides moral or physical strength, freedom of action, or will to act."

As a corollary, Dr. Joe Strange, formerly of the Marine Corps University, has developed a well-regarded model that helps attack an enemy's center of gravity. It is known as the CG-CC-CR-CV analysis, summarized below.

Centers of gravity (CG) are physical or moral entities that are the primary components of physical or moral strength, power, and resistance. They don't just contribute to strength; they *are* the strength. They offer resistance. They strike effective (or heavy) physical or moral blows. At the strategic level, they are usually leaders and populations determined to prevail. At operational and tactical levels, they are almost invariably specific military forces.

Critical capabilities (CC): Every center of gravity has some primary ability (or abilities) that makes it a center of gravity in the context of a given scenario, situation, or mission. Most simply stated: What can this center of gravity do to you that puts great fear (or concern) into your heart in the context of your mission and level of war? The key word in the answer is the verb: it can destroy something, or seize an objective, or prevent you from achieving a mission.

Critical requirements (CR) are conditions, resources, and means that are essential for a center of gravity to achieve its critical capability.

Critical vulnerabilities (CV) are those critical requirements or their components that are deficient or are vulnerable to neutralization or defeat in a way that will contribute to a center of gravity failing to achieve its critical capability. Critical vulnerabilities may be of the silver-bullet type, so that success can be achieved by focusing on just a single vulnerable critical requirement. But more typically, final success can be achieved only by focusing on a combination of vulnerable critical requirements that can be neutralized, interdicted, or attacked simultaneously or sequentially.

The Relevant Critical Requirement

There have been scores of well-researched papers written by the best and brightest in the military regarding the most recent wars in Afghanistan and the Middle East. Any research into the enemy's strategic center of gravity is illuminating, but two papers written by Marine lieutenant colonels at the US Army War College very soon after 9/11—one by James Reilly in 2002, the other by Stephen Davis in 2003—stand out. Because of the date these papers were written, their analyses refer to al-Qaeda, but they are equally applicable to ISIS/ISIL.

In 2002, Lt. Col. James Reilly wrote, "The strategic level center of gravity for al Qaeda is its RADICAL ISLAMIC FUNDAMENTALIST IDEOLOGY" (his emphasis). "This belief constitutes the spirit that permeates throughout the terrorist network and is the cornerstone and justification for their actions. Conveyed by sacred text and imparted via clerical authorities, this radical interpretation of Islamic fundamentalist ideology serves as the legitimizing and enduring force."[1] In 2003, Lt. Col. Stephen Davis wrote, "The Jihadist ideology of al-Qaeda is the center of gravity."[2]

It is very clear how the United States military views the enemy's strategic center of gravity. Using a basic analysis of Dr. Strange's CG-CC-CR-CV model, one might conclude the following:

- *Center of gravity*: Radical Islamic Fundamentalist Ideology
- *Critical capability*: Ability to conduct military and terrorist operations and to recruit believers who will execute their missions.
- *Critical requirement*: Money from various sources, with the vast majority gleaned from the sale of oil.
- *Critical vulnerability*: The technical ability and political will of the Western world to move away from oil as the primary transportation fuel, rendering the export of oil from the Middle East unnecessary.

I believe this would be a valid analysis. Others may reach a different conclusion, but there is little doubt that oil money is critical to funding terrorism.

The Military View of the Critical Requirement

In light of the above analysis, I found the following passages very illuminating—particularly considering the timeframe in which they were written.

Lt. Col. Reilly on some of the money sources: "Direct contributions are a vital source. Supporters across the Middle East donate to bin Laden. According to investigators and intelligence officials, some wealthy Saudi businessmen and some Middle East countries make protection payments to prevent terrorist attacks. . . . An international network of Islamic charities provides millions of dollars, sometimes without the knowledge of charity officials, investigators say. In some cases, the charities are legitimate organizations that allegedly have one or more branches infiltrated by al Qaeda members."[3]

Lt. Col. Davis on money sources: "A great deal of al-Qaeda's power derives from their extensive financial assets and the network that continues to supply them with funding from and through mosques, websites, charities, banks, governmental and non-governmental organizations. . . . While some of the contributions are unintentionally diverted from legitimate causes, many donors are fully aware that their contributions are going to finance terrorist operations. In 2002, the Central Intelligence Agency tracked millions of dollars worth of fund transfers between Saudi Arabia and al-Qaeda and identified 12 prominent businessmen with ties to the Royal family as key backers."[4]

Since great wealth in the Middle East is a result of oil exports, clearly the sources of contributions cited in both of these papers are derived from oil revenue.

Lt. Col. Davis also wrote the following in 2003, before many of today's advanced transportation technologies had been developed:

> The most significant contribution the United States could make using the economic element of national power is to undertake the research required to develop alternate energy sources and develop an implementation plan that would wean the United States from fossil fuel dependency. This is a completely self-contained initiative that this country can implement in a relatively short period of time if it is made a national imperative with appropriate resources

Figure 2.1.

dedicated to its fulfillment. . . . In addition to the development of alternate energy sources, designing more efficient, lighter vehicles could further reduce this consumption considerably within a few years. The dependence of America and the Western world on petroleum and natural gas has held the West hostage to the stability of the Middle East and the demands of extremists for too long.

Again, he said this in 2003. His remarks align with the critical vulnerability described above. Here is what Lt. Col. Davis was talking about: a true reduction in demand. Figure 2.1 is a picture of the mileage on my 2017 Chevy Volt. Notice the number on the lower left, denoting the overall miles per gallon (239) for the lifetime of the vehicle. About 53 miles of pure electric transportation are available before the gasoline engine takes over, if necessary. As will be explained later in the book, 53 miles is more than the average person drives in a day. To charge, I simply plug in to the 110V outlet in my garage, and it charges overnight. Since the last full charge, I drove 102.7 miles on electricity and 5.6 miles on gasoline (just one-tenth of a gallon). Overall, 239 miles per gallon is significantly better than the 20 to 25 miles per gallon that most people get from their vehicles.

The vast majority of miles I drive are purely electric miles, and combined with the little bit of gasoline that I do use, I get *ten times* the miles per gallon that the average vehicle gets. If there are occasional long trips, that number can be five times the miles per gallon. Those numbers make a difference. Hybrids that get forty to fifty miles per gallon are nice, but they don't move the strategic needle. Pure electric miles or some other alternative to oil-based fuel is necessary to make a true difference.

Since 70 percent of oil is used for transportation, most of us getting ten times the mileage or using all electric miles for all trips will change the world. Strategic leverage will shift. Terrorism funding will be reduced. We won't need to send troops to protect the oil infrastructure around the world. This technology is available now, but most people today don't know how far transportation technology has moved forward.

But it is very clear that the military understands. Remember that the board of SAFE (Securing America's Future Energy) includes more than a dozen retired *four-star* generals and admirals. That is a clear signal to all who decide policy on the federal level. We should listen to them not just because they are right but also because they are the ones whom our nation is sending into battle to maintain a status quo that is becoming less and less necessary.

Notes

1. James Reilly, *A Strategic Level Center of Gravity Analysis on the Global War on Terrorism* (Carlisle, PA: Strategy Research Project, US Army War College, 2002).

2. Stephen W. Davis, *Center of Gravity and the War on Terrorism* (Carlisle, PA: Strategy Research Project, US Army War College, 2003).

3. Reilly, *A Strategic Level Center of Gravity Analysis on the Global War on Terrorism,* 11–12.

4. Davis, Center of Gravity and the War on Terrorism, 27–28.

3   What Are the Costs?

THE COSTS OF maintaining an oil-based transportation system are enormous, and there are so many ways in which we continue to pay that burden. Terrorists give many reasons for their attacks against us, but without oil money flowing to the Middle East, carrying out any attack would be difficult, if not impossible. There is a reason the United States has bombed oil convoys belonging to ISIS: their destruction interferes with the flow of money to ISIS.

The information that follows sticks to largely acknowledged facts and was gleaned from multiple news sources such as CNN.com, NBC.com, and History.com (unless otherwise acknowledged) that are readily available to any-one wishing to learn more.

The Human Toll

Here is a short list of some of the more high-profile wars, conflicts, and terrorist incidents that have occurred around the world over the last forty years, followed by some narrative about each. It is difficult to address complex situations through such discrete accounts, but I have described each event simply, understanding that it is the larger narrative that is important.

- The takeover of the American Embassy, Tehran, Iran, 1979
- The bombing of the American Embassy, Beirut, Lebanon, 1983
- The bombing of the US Marine Barracks and French Barracks, Beirut, Lebanon, 1983
- The Persian Gulf War of 1990–91
- The World Trade Center bombing, New York City, 1993
- The bombing of the Saudi military installation, Riyadh, 1995
- The bombing of Khobar Towers, Dhahran, Saudi Arabia, 1996
- The East African embassy bombings, 1998
- The bombing of the USS *Cole*, Aden, Yemen, 2000
- 9/11
- The Global War on Terrorism and Overseas Contingency Operations
- European attacks

The Takeover of the American Embassy, Tehran, Iran, 1979

Susan Chun said, "This conflict is often described as the United States' first brush with political Islam."[1] The following article, published online by PBS (as part of the American Experience series, courtesy WGBH Educational Foundation), is a succinct and illuminating summary of this incident. It should be noted that the United States and its allies' original and primary interest in Iran was its oil.

The Iranian Hostage Crisis

NOVEMBER 1979–JANUARY 1981

On November 4, 1979, an angry mob of young Islamic revolutionaries overran the US Embassy in Tehran, taking more than 60 Americans hostage. "From the moment the hostages were seized until they were released minutes after Ronald Reagan took the oath of office as president 444 days later," wrote historian Gaddis Smith, "the crisis absorbed more concentrated effort by American officials and had more extensive coverage on television and in the press than any other event since World War II."

THE UNITED STATES AND IRAN

The hostage crisis was the most dramatic in a series of problems facing Americans at home and abroad in the last year of the Carter presidency. Was Carter to blame for allowing it to happen? It's hard to say, since the hostage crisis was merely the latest event in the long and complex relationship between the United States and Iran.

Ever since oil was discovered there in 1908, Iran had attracted great interest from the West. The British played a dominant role there until World War II, when the Soviet Union joined them in fighting to keep the Germans out. Until 1953, the United States mostly stayed on the sidelines, advocating for an independent Iran under the leadership of the young king, Reza Shah Pahlavi. But that year, fearing that charismatic prime minister Mohammed Mossadegh might be moving Iran closer to Moscow, the CIA directed an operation to oust him and consolidate power under the Shah.

With a steady flow of oil from the ground and military equipment from the United States, the Shah led Iran into a period of unprecedented prosperity. But growing resentment against an uneven distribution of wealth and the Westernizing influence of the United States led to a confrontation with Islamic clergy in 1963. The Shah effectively put down the uprising, sending its leader, an elderly cleric named Ruhollah Khomeini, into exile in Iraq. Though no one knew it at the time, Iran's Islamic revolution had begun.

THE IRANIAN REVOLUTION

Fast forward to New Years Eve, 1977: President Carter toasted the Shah at a state dinner in Tehran, calling him "an island of stability" in the troubled Middle East. What the president also knew, but chose to ignore, was that the Shah was in serious trouble. As opposition to his government mounted, he had allowed his secret police, SAVAK, to crack down on dissenters, fueling still more resentment. Within weeks of Carter's visit, a series of protests broke out in the religious city of Qom, denouncing the Shah's regime as "anti-Islamic."

The popular movement against the Shah grew until January 16, 1979, when he fled to Egypt. Two weeks later, thousands of Muslims cheered Khomeini's return to Iran after fourteen years in exile.

Did the Carter administration "lose" Iran, as some have suggested? Gaddis Smith might have put it best: "President Carter inherited an impossible situation—and he and his advisers made the worst of it." Carter seemed to have a hard time deciding whether to heed the advice of his aggressive national security advisor, Zbigniew Brzezinski, who wanted to encourage the Shah to brutally suppress the revolution, or that of his more cautious State Department, which suggested Carter reach out to opposition elements in order to smooth the transition to a new government. In the end he did neither, and suffered the consequences.

THE CRISIS

Even after it became known that the Shah was suffering from cancer, President Carter was reluctant to allow him entry to the United States, for fear of reprisal against Americans still in Iran. But in October, when the severity of the Shah's illness became known, Carter relented on humanitarian grounds. "He went around the room, and most of us said, 'Let him in,'" recalls Vice President Walter Mondale. "And he said, 'And if [the Iranians] take our employees in our embassy hostage, then what would be your advice?' And the room just fell dead. No one had an answer to that. Turns out, we never did."

When students overran the embassy and seized more than sixty Americans on November 4, it was not at all clear whom they represented or what they hoped to achieve. In fact, a similar mob had briefly done the same thing nine months earlier, holding the American ambassador hostage for a few hours before members of Khomeini's retinue ordered him released. But this time, Khomeini saw a chance to consolidate his power around a potent symbol, and issued a statement in support of the action against the American "den of spies." The students vowed not to release the Americans until the U.S. returned the Shah for trial, along with billions of dollars they claimed he had stolen from the Iranian people.

CARTER'S RESPONSE

President Carter felt the plight of the hostages deeply, and considered their safe return his personal responsibility. On November 11, he embargoed Iranian oil. On the 17th, Khomeini announced that female, African American, and non-US citizen hostages would be released, because women and minorities already suffered "the oppression of American society." Fifty-three Americans (including two women, Elizabeth Ann Swift and Kathryn Koob, and one African American, Charles Jones) remained as hostages.

Deciding military action was too risky, Carter tried to build pressure on Iran through economic sanctions, and froze its assets in the U.S. While Secretary of State Cyrus Vance led the official diplomatic effort, Hamilton Jordan spent thousands of hours working secret channels. For the first few months, the American public rallied around Carter, who had clearly made freeing the hostages his number one priority. "Having a crisis, where you have to stay in Washington and deal with this crisis all the time, and be a statesman, can work to your advantage—rally around the president in a crisis," says political scientist Betty Glad. "What Carter didn't foresee is, this enormous investment means you have to have a resolution to the issue."

As winter turned to spring, and negotiations failed to produce a deal, frustrated Americans demanded stronger action. "No one can know how much pressure there was on Jimmy to do something," Rosalynn Carter recalled. "I would go out and campaign and come back and say, 'Why don't you do something?' And he said, 'What would you want me to do?' I said, 'Mine the harbors.' He said, 'Okay, suppose I mine the harbors, and they decide to take one hostage out every day and kill him. What am I going to do then?'"

DESERT ONE

Finally, with the Iranians showing no signs of releasing the hostages, Carter decided to take a risk. On April 11, 1980, he approved a high-risk rescue operation, called "Desert One," that had been in the works for months. Though the odds were against its success, the president was devastated when he had to abort the mission due to three malfunctioning helicopters. When another helicopter crashed into a C-130 transport plane while taking off, eight servicemen were killed and three more were injured. The next morning, gleeful Iranians broadcast footage of the smoking remains of the rescue attempt, a stark symbol of American impotence.

THE HOSTAGES' RELEASE

Relatively little happened during the summer, as Iranian internal politics took its course. In early July, the Iranians released hostage Richard Queen, who had developed multiple sclerosis. In the States, constant media coverage—yellow ribbons, footage of chanting Iranian mobs, even a whole new television news program, ABC's Nightline—provided a dispiriting backdrop to the presidential election season. As Carter advisor and biographer Peter Bourne put it, "Because people felt that Carter had not been tough enough in foreign policy, this kind of symbolized for them that some bunch of students could seize American diplomatic officials and hold them prisoner and thumb their nose at the United States."

Finally, in September, Khomeini's government decided it was time to end the matter. There was little more advantage to be gained from further anti-American, anti-Shah propaganda, and the ongoing sanctions were making it harder to straighten out an already chaotic economy. Despite rumors that Carter might pull out an "October Surprise" and get the hostages home before the election, negotiations dragged on for months, even after Republican Ronald Reagan's landslide victory in November. Carter's all-night effort to bring the 52 hostages home before the end of his term, documented by an

ABC television crew in the Oval Office, fell short; the Iranians released them minutes after Reagan was inaugurated.

On January 21, 1981, now-former President Carter went to Germany to meet the freed hostages on behalf of the new president. It was a difficult moment, fraught with emotion. Hamilton Jordan recalled that Carter "looked as old and tired as I had ever seen him."

Susan Chun concluded her article, "The embassy in Tehran is now an Islamic cultural center and a museum, preserved from the days when it was a prison in 1979. It stands as a symbol of the Iranian revolution, and is known in Iran as the 'den of spies.' Old typewriters, communication equipment, even old visa photos, are on display. Every year on the anniversary of the hostage taking, Iranians hold rallies where 'Death to America' is chanted, just as it was in 1979."[2]

The Bombing of the American Embassy, Beirut, Lebanon, 1983

In an attempt to maintain stability in the Middle East, the United States and other Western countries intervened in the Lebanese Civil War. President Reagan sent Marines to Lebanon in 1982 as part of that multinational peacekeeping mission. Their presence was not welcomed by Islamists.

The April 18, 1983, Beirut embassy attack was a dramatic, violent step up from just holding hostages in 1979 in Tehran. It was a suicide bombing that killed sixty-three people, including seventeen Americans. The van carrying the bomb is thought to have been bought in Texas and shipped to the Middle East. It gained access to the embassy compound and parked at the very front of the building, where it exploded. The victims were mostly embassy and CIA staff members but included several US soldiers and one US Marine security guard.

A pro-Iranian group took responsibility for the bombing. However, on May 30, 2003, Judge Royce Lamberth of the US District Court in Washington, DC, determined that the bombing was carried out by the militant group Hezbollah with the approval and financing of senior Iranian officials. Hezbollah is an Islamist militant group based in Lebanon that was originally organized and trained by Iran.

As a continuing sign of instability in Lebanon, when the US embassy was moved to a supposedly more secure location in east Beirut, another car bomb exploded at this embassy location, killing twenty Lebanese and two American soldiers on September 20, 1984.

The April 1983 bombing was only one of the now more common suicide attacks in the region. Other suicide car bombings over the next eight months included one against the US and French embassies in Kuwait. However, an attack that shocked the world was just a few months away.

Figure 3.1. Aftermath of the American Embassy bombing. Source: Alamy

The Bombing of the US Marine Barracks and the French Barracks, Beirut, Lebanon, 1983

After the bombing at the US embassy in April, the security situation in Lebanon continued to deteriorate, as the multinational peacekeeping force that included units from France, Italy, and the United Kingdom took constant attacks. The US positions at the Beirut International Airport were no exception.

Despite the attacks and counterattacks of mortar and rocket fire throughout 1983, the Marines still were under restrictive rules of engagement regarding the use of weapons. (The military is not fond of restrictive rules of engagement, which are usually more political in nature and often fail to match the actual military/security situation.) According to after-action reports, on October 23, 1983, the day of the bombing, those on post were allowed a loaded magazine inserted in their weapon, bolt closed, weapon on safe, with no round in the chamber. This means that an immediate response was not possible if any danger suddenly arose. In fact, when the truck carrying the bomb that would cause so much devastation was speeding its way toward the building, only one Marine had chambered a round in his rifle. The truck actually crashed into the lobby of the building housing the Marines.

The suicide bomber was an Iranian national. The force of the explosion collapsed the four-story building, killing 241 American servicemen. This was the deadliest attack against US Marines since the battle over Iwo Jima in February 1945.

Figure 3.2. Aftermath of the Marine Barracks bombing. Source: Alamy

Figure 3.3. Marine Barracks bombing. Source: Alamy

Figure 3.4. Aftermath of the French Barracks bombing. Source: Alamy

According to Eric Hammel in his book, *The Root: The Marines in Beirut, August 1982-February 1984*, "The force of the explosion initially lifted the entire four-story structure, shearing the bases of the concrete support columns, each measuring fifteen feet in circumference and reinforced by numerous one-and-three-quarter-inch steel rods. The airborne building then fell in upon itself. A massive shock wave and ball of flaming gas was hurled in all directions."[3]

Less than ten minutes later, a similar attack occurred against the French barracks in West Beirut. Although it is believed that the truck did not actually reach the barracks, the explosion still brought down the building, killing fifty-eight French servicemen. It was France's worst military loss since the end of the Algerian War in 1962.

The United States determined that a group tied to Hezbollah, backed by Iran and Syria, was responsible for these bombings. A group named "Islamic Jihad" claimed credit for the bombings, but most observers believe that was a cover name, since Hezbollah did not announce their existence until 1985. Iran continues to deny involvement in the bombings; however, they did erect a monument in Tehran to commemorate the 1983 bombings.

In an after-action report, the Marines were criticized for having lax security at the barracks. The United States withdrew from Lebanon in February 1984, less than two years after arriving.

The Persian Gulf War of 1990–91

Almost all of the other events in this chapter were in some way funded by, or related to, the sale of oil. However, the Gulf War was a massive, definitive statement by the West, defending not only its access to oil but also the necessity of the entire world having access to Middle Eastern oil. The quotes from Secretary Baker and Senator Lugar (page 7) confirm this clearly. This war was about oil. I was there.

Iraq's Saddam Hussein invaded Kuwait on August 2, 1990. He was fresh from an eight-year war with Iran, but he wanted access to the oil resources in Kuwait to force cancellation of debts owed and to control more of the global oil market. His forces moved quickly through the tiny nation, and they consolidated their positions within days.

The reaction around the world was swift. The United States, the Soviet Union, and Great Britain immediately denounced the invasion. On August 3, the United Nations Security Council called for Iraq to withdraw from Kuwait. On August 6, Saudi Arabia requested military assistance from the United States. On August 8, the United States Air Force and NATO troops arrived in Saudi Arabia along with troops from Egypt and other Arab nations. If Hussein was counting on Arab support, he had miscalculated badly. Two-thirds of the twenty-one members of the Arab League condemned the invasion.

Why such quick action? If Iraq could fight Iran for eight years, then invade Kuwait two years later, would Saudi Arabia be next? With the vast oil reserves in Saudi Arabia so necessary to the global economy, combined with the relative stability of the Saudi government, the world could not allow an invasion of that country. The rapid buildup of multinational forces in the northern portions of Saudi Arabia made that very clear.

The economic world order was at stake, and oil was the key.

On November 29, the United Nations Security Council ordered Iraq out of Kuwait by mid-January, but Hussein did not comply. Instead, he eventually increased the Iraqi forces in Kuwait up to three hundred thousand troops. The coalition forces arrayed against him numbered more than seven hundred thousand, including over five hundred thousand from the United States. The coalition included forces from Saudi Arabia, France, Germany, Britain, Japan, Egypt, Syria (yes, Syria)—more than two dozen countries overall. Iraq was aligned with Jordan (oddly), the Sudan, Yemen, and a few others, including the Palestine Liberation Organization. The estimate on the number of casualties in the first few days for the coalition forces was around ten thousand. Coalition members discussed the possibility that Iraq would employ chemical warfare. US forces were taking pills they had never heard of before in anticipation of this kind of warfare. The world was very much on edge.

Figure 3.5. Gas masks were a major focus of the Persian Gulf War. Source: Alamy

When I first arrived in theater in December 1990 as part of my battalion's advance party, I was briefed on our original mission. I'll never forget that briefing. We were to attach our unit to a single Marine division that would attack north through a heavily fortified minefield, defeat eleven Iraqi divisions, and then be prepared to turn west to help the Army. That sort of briefing will get one's attention.

On January 17, 1991, the coalition started its offensive with a United States–led air attack. (We called it "the Air War." Such an operation is standard when a nation has air superiority.) The coalition first took out any air defenses to make subsequent attacks even easier, and then the communications networks so that the Iraqis effectively couldn't talk to each other. Once those two objectives were met, then the standard targets of weapons production facilities, supplies, troop formations, and the like were much easier to attack.

The air operation, lasting just over thirty days, had a devastating effect on the Iraqi forces. Before any ground attack, commanders always want to "soften up" the enemy with either air or artillery attacks. In this case, the strategy worked extremely well.

In concert with the air operations, the overall ground plan was changed with General Norman Schwarzkopf's Left Hook strategy, when he ordered the bulk of the armored troops far west while he kept coalition amphibious forces (US Marines) in the Gulf to keep the Iraqis in place along the Saudi/Kuwaiti border. With the effectiveness of the air attack, this strategy was enormously successful.

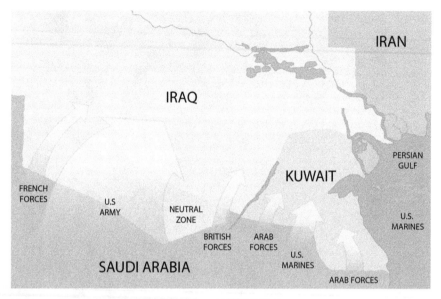

Map 3.1.

Figure 3.6. Highway of Death/Persian Gulf War. Source: Alamy

Saddam Hussein set many of his oil wells on fire during the war. The massive oil cloud that formed moved south, to our position, for three full days. It is difficult to explain this phenomenon. Oil was all around us, at ground level—little oil droplets hanging in the air. It was pitch-black all day long, as we could see only a very few feet in front of us. Normal activities like eating and brushing our teeth were difficult. Environments like this help to explain why many veterans have lingering health issues.

Figure 3.7. Kuwaiti Oil Wells on Fire. Source: Alamy

The ground attack was over in one hundred hours. The buildup of forces began in August 1990, the attack began with air operations on January 17, the ground attack began on February 24, and a ceasefire was declared on February 28. It was almost textbook.

There has been some criticism that Schwarzkopf committed too many forces out west, making the operation risky. But I can attest that as part of this move, our unit, along with hundreds of others, moved either west or east just a few miles south of the Saudi/Kuwaiti border. This created a massive dust cloud for weeks, but it drew no response from Iraq. Presumably, the air operations took out the "eyes" of the Iraqis. They couldn't see it.

What should be obvious is that whatever risk was involved in the strategy, lives were saved as a result. Although all death in war is horrible, the early estimates of ten thousand casualties for the coalition forces never came close to reality. Fewer than four hundred troops from the coalition forces lost their lives. The Iraqis did not fare as well.

There were other incidents in Iraq soon after this war. There was a Kurdish uprising in northern Iraq that was brutally suppressed by Hussein, and United Nations weapons inspectors were also sometimes denied access by Iraq, in spite of previous agreements.

However, the most ominous turn of events was that Osama bin Laden (leader of al-Qaeda), angry that Western troops were allowed into Saudi Arabia, turned his attention away from Russia (in retaliation for invading Afghanistan) to the United States and its allies. Terrorism targeting the United States was about to escalate dramatically, all because we defended oil supplies in the Middle East.

The World Trade Center Bombing, New York City, 1993

As a precursor to 9/11, on February 26, 1993, Islamic terrorists exploded a twelve-hundred-pound bomb in an underground parking garage of the World Trade Center with the intent of toppling the North Tower into the South Tower, thereby bringing both buildings down. In a rather simple plot, the terrorists loaded their powerful homemade bomb into a Ford Econoline van they had rented from a Ryder dealership in New Jersey, and then drove across the Hudson River into Manhattan and the World Trade Center's basement parking garage. They lit four twenty-foot fuses, got into a car that had trailed them, and then sped off.

The 110-story buildings, with tens of thousands of workers in each, were not brought down, but six people died and over a thousand were injured. The explosion created a hole two hundred feet by one hundred feet, several stories deep. An estimated fifty thousand people were evacuated, and the buildings were closed for about a month.

There had been some worries about security surrounding the buildings and possible terrorism threats, but little was done. At this time, most people thought such an incident was unimaginable on US soil. However, related plots also were uncovered to blow up the George Washington Bridge, the United Nations Headquarters, and other New York City landmarks.

FBI agents arrested Mohammad Salameh, who had rented the van under his own name, then—incredibly—returned to the Ryder dealership to ask for his $400 deposit back. He and his three partners were each sentenced to life behind bars. Ramzi Yousef, who organized the bombing and also was arrested, said during his trial, "I am a terrorist and proud of it." He also will remain behind bars for the rest of his life.

Eight years later, a much more tragic terrorist incident—one that would change the course of history—would occur at the same location. However, many more incidents would occur between the 1993 World Trade Center bombing and 9/11.

Figure 3.8. World Trade Center bombing 1993. Source: FBI

The Bombing of the Saudi Military Installation, Riyadh, 1995

Decrying the presence of United States troops in Saudi Arabia, in August 1995 Osama bin Laden wrote an open letter to Saudi leader King Fahd, calling for a guerrilla campaign to drive the US forces out of the kingdom. On November 13 of the same year, a truck bomb (maybe two) exploded outside a Saudi Arabian National Guard Center that was being used by American personnel. Five Americans were killed.

Several groups claim credit for the bombing, but most believe this was the work of bin Laden and al-Qaeda. Four Saudi men, all self-described disciples of bin Laden, were believed to have been executed before the FBI could determine their ties to al-Qaeda.

The Bombing of Khobar Towers, Dhahran, Saudi Arabia, 1996

Khobar Towers, a multiple-building complex, was being used as quarters by multinational forces assigned to conduct a no-fly zone operation in southern Iraq, declared after the Gulf War of 1990–91. On June 25, 1996, a truck bomb was detonated near the eight-story Building #131, which housed US Air Force personnel. Nineteen US service members were killed, and several hundred multinational forces were wounded. The bomb was estimated at five thousand pounds (whereas the bomb used at Riyadh months earlier was estimated at two hundred pounds).

Figure 3.9. Aftermath of the Khobar Towers bombing. Source: Alamy

Since the attackers could not enter the compound, they drove to a parking lot adjacent to Building #131. A chain-link fence around the compound was about seventy feet from the building. The men parked the bomb truck next to the fence and left in another vehicle. The bomb exploded a few minutes later, at approximately 10:20 p.m. local time. It damaged or destroyed six high-rise apartment buildings in the complex. The blast was so powerful that it was felt twenty miles away.

The previous terrorist incident at Riyadh put the Khobar Towers complex on heightened alert, and suspicious activity near the perimeter fences of Khobar Towers was noted by United States Air Force security forces. Also, as noted above, terrorist forces made it known they intended to drive the US forces out of Saudi Arabia. However, the multinational forces were forbidden by the Saudi government to act in any capacity outside the perimeter of the compound, meaning that terrorists could easily carry out surveillance. Much like the attacks of the barracks in Lebanon, security was never adequate to the threat.

Some US officials believe that an Iranian-backed Saudi Hezbollah terrorist group was responsible for the attack, but others believe that bin Laden and al-Qaeda were responsible, especially given that less than a year before, bin Laden had made it known he wanted all US forces out of Saudi Arabia. There is a school of thought that the Saudi government did not want to admit publicly that there were terrorist forces originating within Saudi Arabia, so they wanted to implicate Iran. Iran, however, has denied any role in the bombing.

Figure 3.10. Aftermath of the East African Embassy bombings. Source: FBI

The East Africa Embassy Bombings, 1998

Almost simultaneously on August 7, 1998, truck bombs exploded outside of the US embassies in Nairobi, Kenya, and Dar es Salaam, Tanzania. In total, 224 people were killed and over forty-five hundred were wounded, the vast majority of the casualties being natives of the two African countries. Al-Qaeda was responsible.

In Nairobi, 213 people died, including twelve Americans, with several thousand injured. The explosion in Nairobi also collapsed a nearby building that contained a secretarial college, killing most of the students and staff; a third building was severely damaged. The Dar es Salaam attack killed eleven and injured eighty-five. The attacks were conducted on the eighth anniversary of the first deployment of American troops to Saudi Arabia for the Persian Gulf War of 1990–91.

American officials were aware of al-Qaeda operations in the area and knew of a possible embassy attack in Nairobi, but did not increase security. The US ambassador did ask the State Department to move the embassy for security reasons, but the request was denied.

More than twenty people are suspected of being involved in the bombings, including a former US Army sergeant.

Figure 3.11. USS *Cole* Attack. Source: Alamy

The Bombing of the USS *Cole*, Aden, Yemen, 2000

On October 12, 2000, al-Qaeda suicide bombers, using a small boat loaded with explosives, ripped a hole in the hull of the USS *Cole* while the destroyer was in port for refueling in Aden, Yemen. The ship stopped en route to helping enforce UN sanctions against Iraq. Seventeen US sailors were killed, five of them only nineteen years old. Thirty-nine others were injured.

Although American intelligence officials knew of threats in Yemen, there was no specific threat against the *Cole*. So no suspicions were raised when the terrorists' small boat approached along with a group of other ships aiding the *Cole* in refueling; they reached the ship unchallenged. Accounts of the incident said both terrorists stood up in the moment before the blast.

Investigating the bombing of the USS *Cole* proved to be difficult because of a hostile Yemeni government. Neither the government nor the military was helpful to US officials who investigated in what was still a dangerous area. Years later, the US judicial system also found Sudan liable for the attack, determining that al-Qaeda could not have carried out this attack without help from the Sudanese government.

According to Lawrence Wright in his book *Looming Tower*, the bombing was a "great victory for bin Laden. Al-Qaeda camps . . . filled with new recruits, and contributors from the Gulf States arrived . . . with petrodollars."

Ten months earlier, al-Qaeda had attempted to attack the Navy destroyer USS *The Sullivans* while it was in port at Aden on January 3, 2000. It was a similar plot, but the boat was so heavy with explosives that it sank before reaching its target.

9/11

Even after all of the terrorist attacks against the United States since the Persian Gulf War of 1990–91, most Americans had never heard of Osama bin Laden or al-Qaeda. That all changed on September 11, 2001.

Early that morning, nineteen terrorists hijacked four planes originating from East Coast airports. Three planes conducted suicide attacks against the two large towers of the World Trade Center in New York City and the Pentagon in Washington, DC. The two World Trade Center towers collapsed as a result of the intense heat of the jet fuel. To this day, only 60 percent of the World Trade Center victims have been positively identified. Other nearby buildings suffered damage also, and fires smoldered for several months after the attacks. At the Pentagon, a large hole was blown into the side of the building. These attacks killed about three thousand people.

This was the equivalent of Pearl Harbor in terms of impact—a direct, devastating attack on the homeland.

There were three major differences, though. First, Pearl Harbor was an attack against military forces; 9/11 was an attack against civilians. Second, the attacker at Pearl Harbor was a country, Japan. The attacker on 9/11, al-Qaeda, was what the military calls a "non-state actor" (not a country). Third, immediate video coverage of the attacks on 9/11 allowed the world to watch the aftermath of the attacks, creating a much more visceral reaction throughout the United States and the world.

The fourth plane was headed toward another high-value target (still unknown) but was brought down by the passengers in a field in Pennsylvania, killing everyone on board. Thanks to the communication technologies of the day, the passengers had realized what was happening. According to History.com: "One of the passengers, Thomas Burnett Jr., told his wife over the phone that 'I know we're all going to die. There's three of us who are going to do something about it. I love you, honey.' Another passenger—Todd Beamer—was heard saying 'Are you guys ready? Let's roll!' over an open line." Amazing courage.

All of the flights were picked because they were bound for California, thereby ensuring there was plenty of fuel still on board when the planes reached their targets. Some of the terrorists had lived in the United States for a while and had taken flight lessons for commercial jets, which allowed them to fly the jets once they subdued the flight crews. Others came to the United States just before 9/11, and their task was to commandeer the plane. They easily slipped knives and box cutters through security.

Figure 3.12. Twin Towers, 9/11. Source: Alamy

Osama bin Laden later claimed credit for the attacks. No one disputed that. The main planner of the attack, Khalid Sheikh Mohammed, had actually received a degree from an American University in 1986. He also originally focused his efforts on the Soviet Union as a result of the invasion of Afghanistan but, like bin Laden, later turned his efforts toward the United States.

The attacks of 9/11 demonstrated to the world that al-Qaeda had global reach. The planning included activities in Malaysia, Germany, and Dubai, as well as flight lessons in the United States, all orchestrated from bin Laden's headquarters in Afghanistan.

On the evening of September 11, President Bush addressed the nation and talked of American resolve. He also said, "We will make no distinction between the terrorists who committed these acts and those who harbor them." His actions over the next few years indicated he meant those words.

The economic impact of the attacks was enormous. The estimated loss in the first month alone was over $100 billion. Congress also approved a $40 billion antiterrorism package and appropriated $15 billion to bail out the airlines that suffered losses because people were less willing to fly after the attacks.

Several actions came about directly as a result of the 9/11 attacks.

Figure 3.13. Pentagon, 9/11. Source: Alamy

- For the first time ever, NATO (the North Atlantic Treaty Organization) invoked Article 5 of its charter, relating to collective self-defense. On October 7, the United States and its allies began Operation Enduring Freedom. As a result, in just a few months the Taliban were driven from the Afghan government, thousands of enemy combatants were either killed or captured, and al-Qaeda was now hiding. The US government also conducted extensive operations around the world to root out sympathizers and others assisting al-Qaeda. However, more than fifteen years later, we still have forces in Afghanistan attempting to stabilize that government and eliminate terrorists. "Mixed success" might be an appropriate term, but al-Qaeda's base of operations certainly was disrupted. Osama bin Laden was killed in May of 2011 in Pakistan by US Navy SEALs.
- The US Department of Homeland Security was formed. It consolidated several agencies under its banner, including the Coast Guard and the Immigration and Naturalization Service.
- Much more rigid security measures at airports have now become part of traveling anywhere in the world. Anyone claiming terrorists haven't changed our lives need only visit any commercial airport.
- There is no need to go into detail about the intelligence failures leading to 9/11. However, there have been extensive modifications and increased measures implemented since the attacks, including

sharing of information among agencies. More than fifteen years later, some of these measures are being questioned for possibly impinging on our civil liberties.

- Some believe that al-Qaeda's influence actually waned after these attacks because the group had miscalculated the American response. After the US withdrawals from Beirut and Somalia and weak responses to the East African embassy bombings, this thinking goes, bin Laden believed that the United States would respond meekly to the attacks of 9/11. That was obviously incorrect. When the Taliban were overthrown, the one government that supported al-Qaeda was gone. Its safe haven eliminated, al-Qaeda has operated differently since.
- President Bush identified an "axis of evil" that included Iran, Iraq, and North Korea. He opened the facility at Guantanamo Bay that would hold terrorists, at one time approaching eight hundred prisoners. He also made it clear that the United States was going to be preemptive in its approach and not just respond to attacks anymore. The main goal was to prevent attacks. Although Operation Enduring Freedom was underway, the Global War on Terrorism was about to expand.

The Global War on Terrorism/Overseas Contingency Operations

I will not get bogged down in the nomenclature of this lengthy, continuing operation, as have so many countries, including the United States and Great Britain. Most understand that the War on Terror began in earnest on September 11, 2001. Certainly, as noted above, many actions were initiated as a result of the bombing of the Twin Towers. President Bush, in a televised address to Congress soon after 9/11, made it clear that this conflict would not end until every terrorist group with a global reach was eliminated. At the time, it was not envisioned that the US military was about to embark on its longest-running conflict in history, assisted by many allies.

The first military action, Enduring Freedom, began on October 7, 2001, less than a month after 9/11, with the attack on Afghanistan. Osama bin Laden and al-Qaeda were using Afghanistan as a safe haven and a base of operations, protected by the Taliban, the brutal ruling political movement that controlled that country. Even though the Taliban were overthrown by December 2001, the United States, more than fifteen years later, still has thousands of troops in Afghanistan as a force against the terrorism originating in that country.

Iraqi Freedom, the full-scale invasion of Iraq, began in March 2003, as the United States and allies believed that Saddam Hussein posed an imminent threat. By April, Baghdad was overthrown. However, troops remained in Iraq until the end of 2011. The War on Terror also included operations in the Philippines, North Africa, and other locations.

Figure 3.14. Our troops are constantly put in dangerous situations in cities. Source: Alamy

Figure 3.15. Urban warfare requires eyes everywhere. Source: Alamy

There were numerous surges, pullbacks, and shifts in priorities. Some allies remained and some left. ISIS/ISIL grew into a well-funded terrorist organization, and although bin Laden was killed in 2011, al-Qaeda still exists. We are still involved in the War on Terror, at a continuing great cost.

More than sixty-five hundred US deaths have occurred as a result of the operations surrounding the War on Terror. The direct operations have cost well in excess of a trillion dollars, and other costs associated with the war exceed another two trillion dollars.[4] The operations continue in Afghanistan along with the normal, robust military presence in the Middle East to ensure the flow of oil.

The War on Terror may not have begun as a direct result of protecting oil, but its lineage from the Persian Gulf War of 1990–91, the war that was directly about oil, is obvious.

European Attacks

Our allies in Europe also have suffered at the hands of terrorists funded by oil. Some of these incidents have been horrific, and these attacks in European cities involved large numbers of civilian deaths.

France

France had three high-profile terrorist attacks in 2015–16.

- In January 2015, two gunmen who identified themselves as being al-Qaeda killed seventeen people and wounded twenty-two at the offices of the magazine *Charlie Hebdo* in Paris. A third gunman, identifying with ISIS, conducted two more shootings at a market during the same time frame.
- In November 2015, coordinated attacks at multiple venues in Paris killed 130 people and wounded more than 350. Shootings, grenade attacks, and suicide bombings contributed to the chaos, including ninety killed at a rock concert. ISIS claimed responsibility.
- An Islamic truck driver ran over people in Nice on Bastille Day (July 14, 2016), killing eighty-six people and injuring more than four hundred. ISIS claimed responsibility.

There was also a string of stabbings by radical Islamists throughout France in 2016, largely inspired by ISIS.

England

London experienced coordinated suicide bombings on July 7, 2005. Three of the bombs exploded on Underground trains (their subway system), and another exploded on a double-decker bus. Fifty-two people were killed, with about seven hundred injured. A videotape was made by some of the bombers mentioning Osama bin Laden and al-Qaeda; however, authorities could not make that direct connection.

Authorities in England have had some success in recent years in thwarting attacks, but in 2017 a pop concert attack in Manchester and two vehicle/knife attacks in London occurred. Over three dozen people were killed in the attacks and hundreds injured. Although a direct link to ISIS is not confirmed as of this writing, ISIS has applauded the attacks and indicated the attackers were fighting on their side.

Belgium

On March 22, 2016, Brussels, Belgium, experienced three bombs exploding in coordination, two at an airport and the other near the headquarters of the European Union. More than thirty people were killed and over three hundred wounded. ISIS took responsibility for the bombings.

The incidents mentioned here are but a small sampling of the total number of terrorist incidents. The vast majority of the attacks either have been attributed to or influenced by al-Qaeda and ISIS. The collective nature of these terrorist incidents has resulted in a staggering loss of life, affecting thousands and thousands of families, who suffered enormous grief as a result of these horrifying acts. The funding for the organization and execution of these attacks largely comes from oil.

Let's never forget what really happens after these incidents (figures 3.16 through 3.19).

Real Dollars

Besides the significant human toll, there are real, significant costs that have been incurred. There can be no doubt that the American taxpayer is paying the lion's share of the cost of ensuring that the flow of oil continues throughout the world. The vast majority of that oil is used for transportation.

- The Gulf War of 1990–91 cost approximately $61 billion, according to the Congressional Research Service. Saudi Arabia helped to pay for this war.
- According to several sources, the United States spends about $70 billion per year just to protect global oil supplies. These are not war-related costs. There are other estimates that are higher.
- The Global War on Terror that began after 9/11 has cost over a trillion dollars.
- The soft costs of the War on Terror, including Veterans Administration claims and loss of productivity, exceed another $2 trillion, according to a Brown University study.[5]

Figure 3.16. Source: Alamy

Figure 3.17. Source: Images of Freedom

Figure 3.18. Source: Alamy

Figure 3.19. Source: Images of Freedom

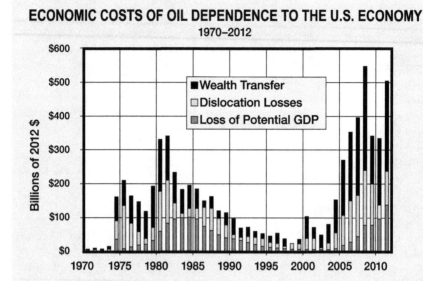

Figure 3.20.

Wealth Transfer is the product of monopoly pricing and price shocks. It is not a loss of GDP but a change in ownership of GDP.

Dislocation Losses are reductions in GDP as a result of oil price shocks.

Loss of Potential Gross Domestic Product (GDP) is the result of producers' and consumers' surplus losses in the oil markets. Our economy could not produce as much as it could have at a lower oil price.

- According to the film *The Burden*, for every one-dollar increase in the price per barrel of oil, the US military spends an additional $130 million. From 2002 to 2008, the military used nearly two billion gallons of fuel in Iraq and Afghanistan.
- The Transportation Security Administration was formed after 9/11 to enhance the safety of travel. Besides the very obvious, inconvenient disruption to travel today compared to that of twenty years ago, the TSA costs over $7 billion per year.
- As recently as 2008–9, imported oil accounted for over half of our trade deficits. Further, almost all economic downturns in the last three decades have had an associated oil price spike. Figure 3.20 is a summary of the economic costs associated with oil dependence by the United States. It is part of a Department of Energy study by

David L. Greene at the Oak Ridge National Laboratory entitled "Measuring the Costs of U.S. Oil Dependence and the Benefits of Reducing It." The dislocation losses (temporary reductions in gross domestic product as a result of oil price shocks) fluctuate, and one can see that the years where that number is significant were years of economic downturn.

It would not be difficult to find significant additional costs if one were to search the federal budget in depth. However, a change to our transportation energy mix would reduce potential future costs greatly—in particular the costs incurred for our military to fight wars and protect the oil infrastructure, along with the dislocation losses illustrated in figure 3.20. The heartbreaking human toll also would lessen if the world would stop sending money to countries that continue to do us harm.

Former Senator Richard Lugar once said that America transfers "hundreds of billions of dollars each year to some of the least accountable regimes in the world." Other nations do the same. We have paid, and continue to pay, a very high price indeed.

A Loss of Strategic Leverage

Finally, there is a loss of strategic leverage by many nations as a result of the world's dependence on oil as a transportation energy source. Let's not forget that OPEC will continue to control the oil market for the foreseeable future, unless transportation technology changes. Its members will direct the oil market to their advantage, not ours—particularly the supply side, in order to manipulate price.

Former Senator Richard Lugar, in an address at Purdue University on August 29, 2006, said, "We have lost leverage on the international stage and are daily exacerbating the problem by participating in an enormous wealth transfer to authoritarian nations that happen to possess the commodity that our economy can least do without. . . . Energy is becoming a weapon of choice for those who possess it."

And former Secretary of State Condoleezza Rice, addressing the Senate Committee on Foreign Relations in 2006, said, "The politics of energy is . . . warping diplomacy around the world."

So, were decisions by the White House or the State Department over the last forty years made in light of our dependence on foreign energy sources? We know that aggressive actions by nations are sometimes tolerated in light of the world's dependence on oil. Europe must tolerate some of Russia's aggression because so much of their energy needs are fulfilled by Russia. China and India have relations with Middle Eastern and North African nations because their still-emerging economies need oil.

In a speech to the Brookings Institution in 2006, Senator Lugar said,

> While staying overnight in the Corinthia Hotel in Tripoli . . . I came face to face with the microcosm of the new reality of global economic life. It was impossible to walk around the hotel without meeting someone who was hoping to tap into Libya's oil reserves. The hotel was populated with representatives from China, India, and Western oil companies who were in Libya to stake out drilling or refining options for every pool of oil that the government might make available. . . . The Chinese and Indians, with one third of the world's people between them, know that their economic future is directly tied to finding sufficient energy resources to sustain their rapid economic growth. They are negotiating with anyone willing to sell them an energy lifeline.

There is much research that confirms the relationship between China and Iran. China not only imports oil from Iran but also has agreements to develop oil and natural gas fields in Iran. In return, China helps Iran with advanced military technology along with nuclear technology. There is a school of thought that both nations see their relationship as a counter to the role of the United States in the Middle East.

India, another rapidly growing economy, is also very dependent on oil from the Middle East. Over half of India's oil imports come from Middle Eastern nations.

This has nothing to do with the concepts of free trade or isolationism. It is simply the loss of strategic leverage that is evident, as Middle Eastern oil will continue to determine bilateral relationships well into the future if we do not change transportation technology.

I am not postulating that previous decisions made at national levels around the world were incorrect or were made without great thought. Decisions made at those levels are extremely difficult, usually with dozens of factors to be taken into account. However, we want future decisions, particularly those that involve the use of armed forces, to be made without the specter of oil dependence as the backdrop.

Again, in his speech to the Brookings Institution, Senator Lugar said, "No one who is honestly assessing the decline of American leverage around the world due to our energy dependence can fail to see that energy is the albatross of US national security."

We can change that.

Notes

1. Susan Chun, "Six Things You Didn't Know about the Iran Hostage Crisis," CNN.com, October 27, 2014, updated July 16, 2015. https://www.cnn.com/2014/10/27/world/ac-six-things-you-didnt-know-about-the-iran-hostage-crisis/index.html.
2. Chun, "Six Things You Didn't Know."

3. Eric Hammel, *The Root: The Marines in Beirut, August 1982-February 1984* (Zenith, St. Paul, MN, 1999), 303.

4. See, for example, Neta C. Crawford, "United States Budgetary Costs of Post-9/11 Wars Through FY2018," (Cost of War study, Watson Institute for International and Public Affair, Brown University, Providence, RI, November 2017).

5. Crawford, "United States Budgetary Costs of Post-9/11 Wars."

4 How Did We Get to This Point?

THANKS TO OUR continuing dependence on oil, we are still in the midst of the greatest voluntary transfer of wealth in world history. Future historians will not judge us kindly. How did this come to be?

The sections in this chapter are basic in their approach but provide sufficient background to understand how we arrived at the current situation. The sections are as follows:

- World War I: The Middle East Becomes Relevant
- Recent History: The Brits Move Out, the Americans Move In
- A Short Story of Oil
- The Development of the Automobile

Appendix D provides a more in-depth analysis of oil and the Middle East. In preparation for this chapter, I asked some specific questions of the Truman Project for National Security; Victoria Gurevich provided a remarkable response. I have summarized her answers for this chapter, but I believe the response was so strong that those wanting more detailed information should be able to avail themselves of her research. In that spirit I have included her complete response in Appendix D.

World War I: The Middle East Becomes Relevant

Early in the twentieth century, the Middle East was largely composed of the Ottoman Empire, the tribes of the Arabian Peninsula, Persia (largely Iran today), and many other Bedouin groups. Connecting the East to the West, the Ottoman Empire occupied present-day Turkey, Iraq, Syria, Lebanon, Israel, Palestine, Jordan, and parts of Saudi Arabia, with Istanbul as its capital city. The Arabian Peninsula was ruled by a patchwork of tribal kingdoms until 1932, when the modern state of Saudi Arabia was established.

Before World War I, there were four major centers of activity in the Arabian Peninsula: the kingdoms of Nejd, Hijaz, Al Hasa, and Asir, operating independently of one another and with infrequent confrontation (unless a conquest was undertaken). With the exception of income from the holy sites of Mecca and Medina in the Hijaz territory, economic activities sustaining the livelihoods of the rest of the Arabian population were predominantly agrarian.

Instead of the rigid borders we know today, the Middle East prior to World War I was loosely bound by national boundaries and administered by tribal

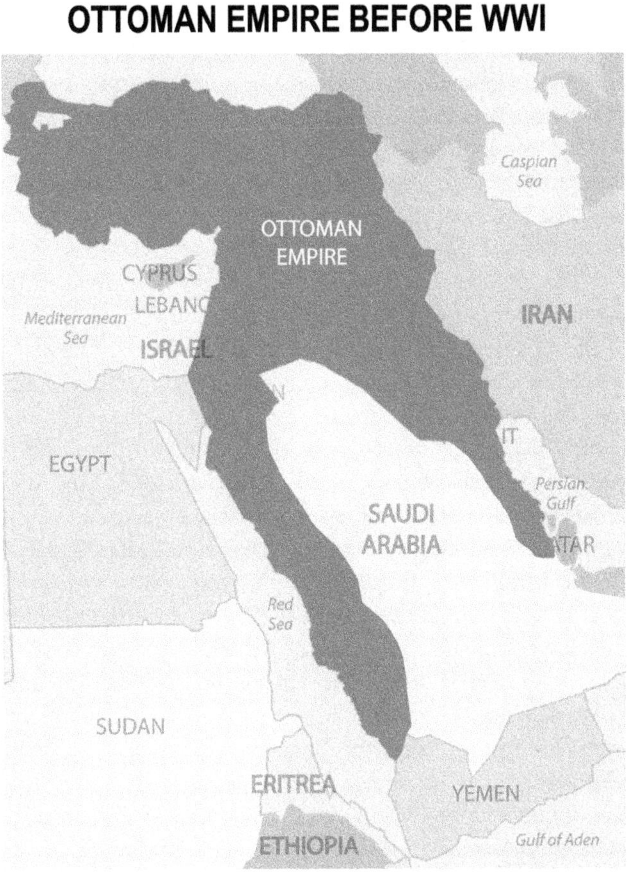

OTTOMAN EMPIRE BEFORE WWI

Map 4.1.

rulers. The seminomadic nature of the majority of Middle Eastern inhabitants at the time determined the economies that supported their existence, with the vast majority of the people in the Middle East living outside large towns, making their living from cultivation, herding, or a combination of the two. This largely land-based, agricultural economy had limited infrastructure, with very little urbanization and very limited external trade. Industry did exist in the more heavily populated areas, such as Istanbul, which often produced goods for export—such as sugar, cigarettes, carpets, and silk thread—mainly for European markets.

It was the dissolution and partition of the Ottoman Empire by world powers, as a result of World War I, that guided the formation of national boundaries in the region, creating much of the national landscape of the Middle East today.

Oil had been discovered prior to World War I (in Persia in 1908, for instance), but oil was not considered essential to economies at the time. Coal largely supported industrial development, and most major industries rebuffed the idea of oil as a primary source of fuel, including the Royal Navy, the dominant military fleet in the world. That was soon to change.

The impetus for change stemmed from the naval race between Britain and Germany, with the latter competing for prominence and the former maneuvering to dominate the world stage. According to Daniel Yergin in *The Prize: The Epic Quest for Oil, Money and Power*, by 1911 the Royal Navy had built or was building large numbers of destroyers and submarines powered by oil, but the battleships—the most important ships—were still powered by coal.

When Winston Churchill joined the Navy as first lord of the admiralty (in a civilian role), he undertook a series of programs in 1912, 1913, and 1914 that introduced entire fleets of ships fed only by oil, "on which our life depended." Churchill's decision to convert to oil raised a serious problem, however, in that the switch was made before a reliable supply of oil had been secured. Eleven days after Parliament approved Churchill's bill to purchase 51 percent of Anglo-Persian, an oil company based in Persia, and sign a twenty-year contract for fuel oil, World War I began. A race to find oil reserves in the region ensued, guided by the need to secure a reliable petroleum source for the Royal Navy. As a result, from 1912 to 1918, oil production in Persia "grew more than tenfold," according to Yergin. The need for oil began to loom large in British military and political planning.

As World War I progressed, the British and French, in a 1916 agreement known as the Sykes-Picot Agreement, preemptively partitioned the region of Mesopotamia, thought to be rich in oil reserves, in anticipation of the dissolution of the Ottoman Empire. For both Britain and France, the ownership and security of reliable oil reserves was a war aim, but it led to disagreement over the delineation of borders.

It wasn't until 1920, at a meeting of the Allied Supreme Council, that an agreement over borders was reached. Known as the San Remo Agreement, Mesopotamia was divided as follows (from *Encyclopedia Britannica*):

> Two "A" mandates were created out of the old Ottoman province of Syria: the northern half (Syria and Lebanon) was mandated to France, the southern half (Palestine) to Great Britain. The province of Mesopotamia (Iraq) was also mandated to Great Britain. Under the terms of an "A" mandate the individual countries were deemed independent but subject to a mandatory power until they reached political maturity. . . . An Anglo-French oil agreement was also concluded . . . providing France with a 25 percent share of Iraqi oil and favorable oil transport terms and stipulating in return the inclusion of Mosul in the British mandate of Iraq.

The Sykes-Picot Agreement was the basis for the founding of Syria, Jordan, Iraq, Lebanon, and Palestine. Britain and France were granted mandates

SAN REMO AGREEMENT

TURKEY

Caspian
Sea

FRENCH
MANDATE

CYPRUS

LEBANON

Mediterranean
Sea

ISRAEL

BRITISH
MANDATE

IRAN

RDAN

EGYPT

IT

Persian
Gulf

SAUDI
ARABIA

QATAR

Red
Sea

SUDAN

ERITREA

YEMEN

Gulf of Aden

ETHIOPIA

Map 4.2.

over their respective territories, which they could administer as desired. Britain appointed governments in Iraq and Jordan, while France appointed the government of Syria and Lebanon. Palestine remained as a British protectorate until 1948.

It is important to note that Britain and France chose to manage their mandates very differently. Ayse Tekdal Fildis, in a 2011 article in *The Middle East Policy Council*, says the following: "Britain's interest in the provinces focused on safeguarding the route to India, securing cheap and accessible oil for the Empire's needs, maintaining the balance of power in the Mediterranean to its advantage, and protecting its financial concerns. France hoped to preserve her centuries-old ties with the Syrian Catholics, gain a strategic and economic base in the eastern Mediterranean, ensure a cheap supply of cotton and silk and prevent Arab nationalism from infecting her North African empire."

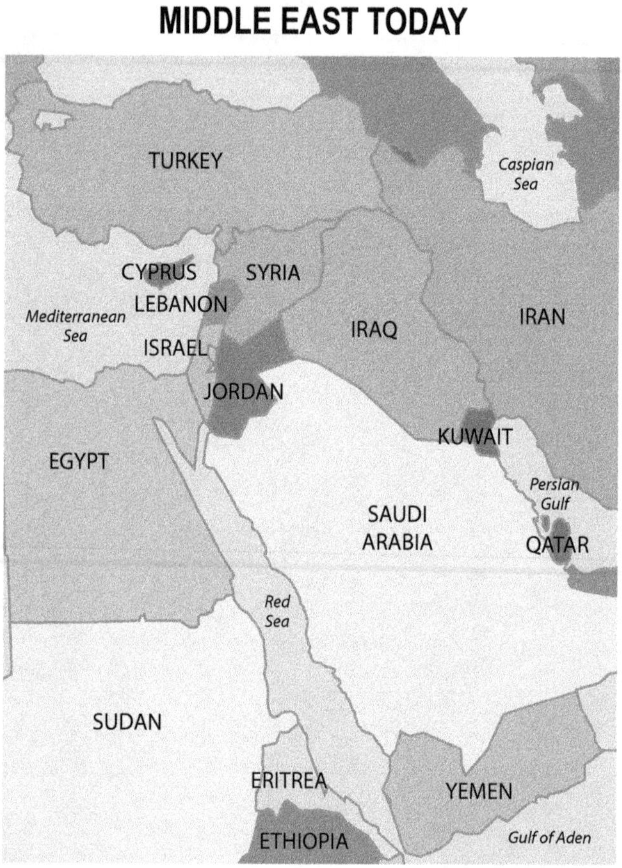

MIDDLE EAST TODAY

Map 4.3.

The neat lines that were drawn by British and French mandates somewhat acknowledged the background of the region but did not anticipate how integral the lines were to maintaining amicability between peoples. The grievances that were felt after the creation of state boundaries differed between each state and developed at different times; however, the majority of the problems plaguing the region today can be traced back to the partitions by Britain and France.

For instance, the territory of Iraq in 1921 comprised diverse groups with little common political or cultural history but with a rising Arab nationalism. Into this arrangement, Britain wished to introduce constitutionalism and parliament. As from the Ottoman Empire, the Sunni Arabs continued to hold political power, despite the Shia being by far the most numerous. Until the British mandate of Iraq was terminated in 1932, British forces played a central and effective role in suppressing Shia and Kurdish rebellions for independence. Once British forces left, however, Iraq experienced a series of rebellions and coups that have left the country in a chronic state of instability. British manipulation of the region spurred the Arab nationalist movements that would resurface in the country and region for decades to come.

Once the French were formally granted their mandate over Syria in 1920, they assumed control over six distinct provinces including Lebanon, and introduced "new national identities, citizenship and social class," all of which challenged and even replaced "the identities of clan, tribe and religion," according to Tekdal. A territory at first, Lebanon was inaugurated as independent from Syria because of the large (although still minority) population of Maronite Christians, whom the French regarded favorably. The borders of Lebanon were constructed so as not to include too many Muslim communities that would threaten the Maronites' position of power. The new country of Lebanon, formed in 1941, was not influenced by the oil industry, as there were no petroleum deposits in the area. Resistance to the divisions introduced as a result of Sykes-Picot did not boil over until 1975, when the Lebanese Civil War erupted. The war was fought over the political influence that the Maronites held amidst a growing Muslim population, and it resulted in the national Muslim majority assuming political power.

While Lebanon was removed from the Greater Syrian mandate, the remaining conglomeration of ethnicities and religious sects was mingled in Syria. Pan-Arab nationalist sentiments were felt early on in Syria, sentiments that the French went to great lengths to suppress. From 1920, when the San Remo Agreement was officially issued, until 1945, when the mandate was over, Greater Syria existed under multiple forms of government that kept Arab political unity at bay. Different administrations governed the numerous ethnic and religious groups that resided in Syria, often reorganizing every couple of years. After Syria was granted independence in 1946, the country suffered numerous military coups and revolts for the next several decades, driven by feelings of disenfranchisement and nationalist sentiments.

Jordan was different, and an anomaly. The population of Jordan was much less varied than it was in other countries; as a result, there was less ethnic and sectarian tension than in Iraq. While a British mandate also existed over the territory of Jordan, the history of this protectorate has proven to be more stable. Oil had little influence in the formation or economic prosperity of Jordan, as the area has no petroleum deposits and relies on imports for all of its energy needs. To this day, Jordan remains one of the most stable nations in the Middle East and has managed to avoid the resistance movements that have taken root in other parts of the region.

It is almost hard to believe that Saudi Arabia, the dominant oil producer for the last half of the twentieth century, did not initially wish for oil to dominate its economy. Abdul Aziz—later known as Ibn Saud—spent the first three decades of the twentieth century conquering Arabia to fulfill his dream of reestablishing the Saudi dynasty. In 1930, Ibn Saud had accomplished his mission of uniting the Arabian Peninsula and commemorated the feat by renaming the area Saudi Arabia.

Fearing a loss of traditional values and relationships, Ibn Saud did not wish to see his country transformed into an oil state. Soon after consolidation, however, the new kingdom was quickly running out of money as a result of the onset of the Great Depression, which significantly reduced the number of pilgrims that were traveling to the holy sites of Mecca and Medina.

Early in the century, oil had yet to be discovered in Saudi Arabia, so selling a concession to search for oil—with no guarantee any was to be found—was a small gamble. Standard Oil won the concession and agreed to pay the king a £30,000 interest-free loan, another £25,000 loan eighteen months later, and £5,000 annually. The concession was administered by the California Arabian Standard Oil Company subsidiary—renamed the Arabian American Oil Company (Aramco) in 1944 after joining with Texas Oil—and was the only exclusively American-owned and -operated petroleum venture in the Middle East.

The United States became involved in Saudi Arabia through its venture in Bahrain. In the late 1920s, Bahrain had been attempting to sell oil concessions; however, according to Yergin, a geological report conducted in Saudi Arabia in 1926 stated that the prospects of oil on the Arabian Peninsula left "little room for optimism." In retrospect, that is amazing. Standard Oil, sensing opportunity, wanted to secure oil resources outside of the United States and won the Bahrain oil concession in 1930. Standard Oil set up a subsidiary company, the Bahrain Petroleum Company, and struck oil in Bahrain in 1932. Bahrain's geology is similar to that of Saudi Arabia, and its oil reserves contradicted the report that had deterred potential prospectors for half a decade. To continue its exploration, Standard Oil turned to Saudi Arabia.

Oil was finally struck in Saudi Arabia in 1938, and when Ibn Saud received a royalty check for $1.5 million, the concession was expanded to over 50 percent of Saudi Arabia. Aramco went from producing 11,000 barrels a day in 1939 to more than 477,000 barrels a decade later—about a third of all Middle East production. Unfortunately, the wealth from the new oil industry was not used to elevate society; rather, Ibn Saud spent his royalties on personal extravagances and political favors. It wasn't until the mid-1960s, under the reign of King Faisal, that reforms and modernization were undertaken in Saudi Arabia.

A report in 1949 revealed that Aramco was paying more to the United States in taxes than it was paying to Saudi Arabia in royalties, a division that was unacceptable to Saudi Arabia. That same year, Saudi Arabia took up negotiations to establish a profit-sharing arrangement, which was reached in 1951 with a fifty-fifty agreement with Aramco. For the next twenty-five years, the arrangement stayed in place. However, thoughts of nationalization brewed below the surface. In 1970, Saudi Aramco—the national company that would eventually take over the foreign-owned Aramco—was formed. Unlike other nationalizations, the handover of Aramco was done gradually, with the king taking over in 1980 and the name of the company being officially changed in 1988. The two countries—the United States and Saudi Arabia—maintained close business relations, with the latter being the owner and the former being the operator. The nationalization of Saudi Aramco strengthened the rentier economy that characterizes Saudi Arabia.[1] The nationalization of Saudi Aramco, in addition to changing the social lives of citizens, also affected political life. By not collecting taxes, the Saudi government was not responsible to its citizens, and political participation and criticism were slowly eradicated.

Interestingly, shortly after the end of World War I, the United States was faced with the threat of exhausting its domestic oil reserves within several decades. While discussions about the prospect of shale oil in the mountains of Colorado, Utah, and Nevada were ongoing, the US oil industries and American government turned their search for oil outward. When news of the San Remo Agreement of 1920 reached the United States, it was denounced as "old fashioned imperialism" and "seemed to violate the principle of equal rights among the victorious Allies," according to Yergin. After diplomatic dialogue between the United States, Britain, and France, all parties agreed that it was in their best interests that American companies be allowed to develop the region.

Recent History: The Brits Move Out, the Americans Move In

So much of the strategic dilemma that the world faces today with oil dates back to agreements made during and after World War I. The Sykes-Picot and San Remo Agreements have been discussed above, but it is important to note that for the first half of the twentieth century, Great Britain was the dominant power in the Middle East, and its role in the Middle East had been as a protector, ensuring that trade routes and oil sources remained undisturbed.

After World War II, however, Britain was faced with "deepening British financial weakness; bruising domestic political debate over the priorities and values of British foreign policy and increasingly intractable and violent nationalist sentiment in the Middle East."[2] Britain announced in 1968 that it was withdrawing its military presence from the Middle East. Without a large naval fleet, it could no longer safeguard global oil interests in the region, a resource that was essential for the entire developed world.

When Britain decided to withdraw from the Persian Gulf, the United States was faced with a strategic dilemma regarding influence in the region. Threatened with Cold War tensions and given the potential power vacuum in the region, the United States wanted to establish a defense against Soviet infiltration into the Middle East. Not wishing to become entangled in the region directly but still wanting to exert influence, President Nixon decided on the "Twin Pillars Strategy," establishing Iran and Saudi Arabia as regional powers—surrogates that would act in accordance with US interests. These "pillars" were encouraged to acquire copious amounts of advanced arms from the US government to support their new roles as "regional policemen."

Soon thereafter came the 1973–74 oil embargo by OPEC (including Saudi Arabia and Iran) and others in response to America's involvement in the 1973 Yom Kippur War, which began with a surprise attack by Egypt and Syria against Israel. Oil prices tripled during the embargo, and OPEC quickly learned that they had enormous strategic leverage. Although there was cooperation with the Twin Pillars, the strategy did not seem to influence cooperation with Saudi Arabia and Iran to the point where diplomacy could prevent the embargo.

When the shah of Iran, long an ally of the United States, was overthrown in January 1979, the Twin Pillars Strategy was dead. While the Twin Pillars Strategy initially was meant to equip regional powers to protect their own resources, thereby making unnecessary any direct US involvement, the strategy instead ushered in a pattern of militarism that contributed to the destabilization of the region that continues to this day.

As a result, there was (and is now) an enormous amount of military equipment in the Middle East. In September 1980, Iraq invaded Iran largely in response to the Iranian Revolution the year before. The conflict lasted eight years and was ended in August 1988 by a ceasefire brokered by the United Nations. No borders were changed nor reparations paid, but it is estimated that half a million soldiers were killed, along with a like number of civilians. It is widely believed that Iraq used chemical munitions during this war.

The Gulf War of 1990–91 followed when more than five hundred thousand troops (I was one of them) deployed as part of an international coalition in response to Iraq's invasion of Kuwait. Iraq invaded primarily in response to a dispute over revenues from the Rumaila oil field.

The international coalition was successful in driving Iraq back, but in response to the large number of Western troops fighting in the Middle East, al-Qaeda leader Osama bin Laden turned his attention from Russia (which began as a result of Russia's invasion of Afghanistan) to the United States and its Western allies. The dramatic increase in terrorism followed and continues to this day, primarily funded by oil revenue.

Part of the irony of the role of oil in the Middle East is that the 1916 Sykes-Picot Agreement, which was designed partially to protect oil supplies for the British, actually produced little oil other than Iraq's. Also, the Arabian Peninsula, originally thought to be of little value regarding oil, became a major producer of oil beginning in the late 1930s. However, the Sykes-Picot and San Remo Agreements did produce Arab nationalist feelings, which became more pronounced throughout the twentieth century, with the prodigious quantities of exported oil fanning the flames.

However, countries in the Middle East have had varying relationships with oil.

Middle Eastern Countries and the Influence of Oil

Iraq—As discussed previously, Sykes-Picot granted the British a mandate over Iraq, chosen for its oil reserves. At the time of the formation of the state, the ethnic and religious composition of Iraq was varied, with political power being concentrated within the Sunni minority group. With that, the revenues from the sale of oil in this rentier economy were concentrated in the minority Sunni population. Iraq had a tumultuous start after the British mandate ended in 1932, making economic development difficult as the country endured numerous coups and revolutions. After a prolonged war with Iran, Iraq invaded Kuwait in 1990 to acquire more oil reserves and thereby incurred the wrath of much of the world. Longtime dictator Saddam Hussein was overthrown by the United States in an invasion after 9/11. Stability has evaded Iraq ever since, and the nation currently is threatened by the expansion of ISIS/ISIL.

Iran—Not involved in the Sykes-Picot agreement, Persia changed its name to Iran in the 1930s. Also a rentier state, Iran has been dependent on oil revenues since the resource was discovered there in 1908. Beginning in 1925, Mohammed Reza Shah began modernizing Iran economically, socially, and culturally. Modernization advanced but left many groups behind, especially the more traditional and rural populations. With the Iranian Revolution in 1979, the dictatorship was passed to a theocratic elite. While state-owned oil revenues fueled growth, they also eliminated government accountability and quelled political participation. Because the state relies on revenues from the sale of natural resources for the majority of its economy, other sectors of society remain underdeveloped. Nevertheless, the economy of Iran is the second largest in the Middle East and North Africa. Iran has been on the US State Department's State Sponsor of Terrorism list since 1984.

Saudi Arabia—This nation boasts the largest economy in the Middle East and North Africa. Saudi Arabia is the definition of a rentier economy and therefore secures significant state revenues from a single industry: oil. Oil revenues in Saudi Arabia are very much responsible for the country's quality of life (although modernization reforms were not undertaken until the 1960s, several decades after wealth from oil revenues became available). The exchange for material wealth as a result of oil revenues is the implicit social contract that buys consent from its citizens.

Lebanon, Syria, Jordan, Palestine—For the other countries that emerged as a result of Sykes-Picot, oil has played a minor role in the development of their economies and society. There are no oil reserves in Lebanon, Jordan, and Palestine, and oil was not discovered in Syria until 1956. The economies of Jordan and Lebanon are emerging markets that have seen promising growth rates in the past decade or so but will be tested by the ongoing regional crisis. While not a major oil producer by Middle East standards, Syria relies on oil revenues to fund a significant portion of its economy.

The current close relationship between Syria and Russia today was established in 1946, when the Soviet Union and the fledgling state of Syria "signed a secret agreement stating that the new nation of Syria would provide diplomatic and political support to the USSR in exchange for military aid and assistance in forming a national army."[3] Syria then became a client state of the Soviet Union during the Cold War and adopted a socialist economic model, closing its economy. What limited the economy further were the imposition of sanctions during the Cold War years by the United States and another wave of sanctions in the mid-2000s.

Bahrain—The first oil discovery on the Arab side of the Gulf was made in Bahrain; however, the supply was small by Middle Eastern standards. Bahrain has diversified its economy so that oil revenues account for a small portion of its economy, while the banking sector has become an active industry. Because of Bahrain's small population, quality of life in the country has been ranked highly, consequently attracting a significant number of non-national employees. Society in Bahrain today represents a mix of nationalities and religions.

Kuwait—After threats from the Ottoman Empire, Kuwait became a British protectorate in 1899. When oil was discovered in Kuwait in 1937, revenues were used to modernize its commercial center and raise the standard of living to the high quality enjoyed today. Kuwait is heavily dependent on its oil, with revenues from the industry accounting for the vast majority of the national budget. As a result of political challenges since the 1990s, necessary economic reforms and diversification projects have gone largely unmet. Unlike other rentier states, Kuwait in recent years has seen increasing political participation and social modernization.

Now you have some background on the historical and political aspects of oil. But what about the commodity itself, and transportation—the technology that depends on it so heavily? They also have a history that explains why the world is in its current situation.

A Short Story of Oil

Much of the story of oil is well known and generic. However, I do include here some details derived from the PBS series *Extreme Oil*. Regarding oil's impact on the automobile, I found Martin Melosi's "Energy Use and the Internal Combustion Engine," from his work *The Automobile and the Environment in American History*, to be helpful.[4]

Oil was created when decayed plants and algae collected on the seabed millions of years ago. Eventually, layer on layer of sediment accumulated on top, creating warmth and pressure that transformed the organic matter into oil. The oil remained beneath the earth, largely untapped, until relatively recently. For thousands of years, humans utilized oil as a lubricant, as an adhesive, and for many other purposes, including medicinal uses. Crude oil and its more viscous form, bitumen, have made their way to the surface of the earth naturally in "oil seeps."

As early as five thousand years ago, ancient Sumerians, Assyrians, and Babylonians used asphalt from seeps along the Euphrates as mortar and for waterproofing, and ancient Egyptians were known to use liquid oil for medicinal purposes and in embalming. Ancient Persian military forces used oil-soaked flaming arrows during the siege of Athens. In North America, Native Americans used tar as an adhesive and to bind stone tools to wooden handles. George Washington's troops used oil to treat frostbite. In 1792, a newspaper ad for "Seneca Oil," named after the Native American tribe, pitched oil as a cure-all tonic to New World settlers. However, through the early nineteenth century, large-scale production and use of oil was unknown.

However, in the nineteenth century, oil and its derivatives became more useful as a source of energy. As early as 1815, several streets in Prague were lit using petroleum lamps. Then in 1849 Canadian geologist Abraham Gesner distilled a new lamp fuel from petroleum, which he called kerosene. This cheaper, cleaner-burning fuel eventually replaced whale oil in lamps. Gesner—though he never became wealthy from his discovery—eventually became known as the "Father of the Petroleum Industry." His invention also has been credited with helping to save the whales.

Kerosene for lamps was the main commercial use of oil for decades, but actively searching for oil did not begin until the Drake Well was drilled in 1859 in northwestern Pennsylvania. Previously, wells were drilled for water or salt brine, and oil was often an unacceptable byproduct of drilling for those products.

This changed as discoveries for uses of oil sprang up across the United States in the late nineteenth century. Such discoveries were paralleled by scientific developments that found more and more uses for petroleum products in an assortment of industries. In 1870, eleven years after the Drake Well was opened, John D. Rockefeller founded Standard Oil primarily for the production of kerosene. By 1878, Standard Oil was responsible for roughly 90 percent of the refining capacity in America.

But also in 1878, Thomas Edison invented the incandescent light bulb. Edison's invention eventually would make the kerosene lamp obsolete and put a damper on oil's commercial flame. However, with the mass production of the automobile on the horizon along with other technological developments, oil production began to flourish.

The oil industry was saved by the use of gasoline, a previously little-used byproduct of the oil refining process. Henry Ford's decision to use gasoline in his mass-produced Model T, introduced in 1908, was key. That revolutionary car made the automobile accessible to many Americans and changed the way we viewed mobility. Eventually, gasoline-powered vehicles changed travel, warfare, and countless other aspects of twentieth-century life, and oil refining became the keystone to the empire of Standard Oil.

As a result, Rockefeller became the world's richest man. On his death in 1937, his wealth was equivalent to 1.5 percent of the national economy. His net worth then, adjusted for inflation, would be well over $300 billion in today's economy.

The middle third of the twentieth century saw tremendous changes in the oil industry. Oil prospecting began a global expansion, beginning with Standard Oil's activities in Saudi Arabia. The internationalization of oil production played an important role in World War II. The Allied forces' access to oil, in fact, was considered a crucial factor in their victory over the Axis powers in World War II.

Because of oil's importance to the future of the nation, oil policy became a high priority at the end of World War II. Oil exploration in North America, which expanded during the early twentieth century, later led to the United States becoming the world's leading producer by mid-century. As petroleum production in the US peaked during the 1960s, however, the United States was surpassed by Saudi Arabia and the Soviet Union.

Meanwhile, scientific discoveries and inventions fueled a market for petroleum products. Robert Banks and fellow research chemist Paul Hogan discovered two new types of plastic, called crystalline polypropylene and high-density polyethylene (HDPE), while working for Phillips Petroleum. The plastics, first marketed under the brand name Marlex, are responsible for many of the common plastic products found today, such as milk jugs, carpeting, and housewares. One of the first uses for Marlex was to make Wham-O hula hoops. Also, Du Pont scientist Wallace Carothers invented nylon, the first purely synthetic fiber, using petroleum-based hydrocarbons.

In 1960, the Organization of Petroleum Exporting Countries formed in Baghdad with five member nations: Iran, Iraq, Kuwait, Saudi Arabia, and Venezuela. There are twelve members today. OPEC was formed when multinational companies dominated the international oil market; thus, the formation of OPEC can be seen as the seminal moment when these nations began to exert sovereignty over their own natural resources. Today, over 80 percent of the oil market is controlled by state agencies, not by corporations.

That control was first exercised forcefully in 1973 when OPEC levied an oil embargo in response to the United States' support of Israel during the Arab-Israeli conflict. Oil prices tripled, and Americans waited in line for hours to fill up their tanks only partially. But the most powerful outcome of the embargo was that OPEC realized the enormous strategic leverage these nations now held over the quality of life of the Western nations and their allies.

Unbelievably, America learned nothing from the embargo. Despite presidential proclamations (see chapter 1), our reliance on foreign oil increased from 28 percent in the early 1970s to 42 percent in the mid-1980s and to 60 percent in the 2000s.

Interestingly, the use of oil by sector changed dramatically during this same time period. Oil use for electricity and heating oil dropped so dramatically that the primary use of oil today is in transportation. It is the global transportation sector alone that keeps enormous sums of money flowing from all over the world to our enemies in the Middle East.

Meanwhile, we not only continue to send troops to fight both state and non-state actors in the Middle East, but, as mentioned, we spend close to $70 billion annually (outside of the costs of war) just to protect the worldwide oil infrastructure that allows the flow of oil around the globe. We do this to maintain our standard of living, so that goods and services can be bought and sold.

However, this means that we actually protect the infrastructure that allows every country to send money to our enemies.

The Development of the Automobile

In the early stages of automobile production, it was not a given that the gasoline-powered internal combustion engine was going to dominate the market. The engine that we use primarily today had stiff competition from both steam-powered and electric-powered cars when the automobile was in its formative stages.

The First Cars Were . . . Steam?

Steam-powered vehicles were originally produced in the late eighteenth century and continued to be built through the nineteenth century, with Great Britain as a center for innovation. They were still seen as a viable mode of transportation early into the twentieth century, when self-propelled vehicles of varying means for power were being developed. Like all vehicles of that time, steam had a number of practical issues to address. The early steamers started up slowly—sometimes up to forty-five minutes in the cold—and ran noisily, had unreliable controls and problems with freezing, and they would need to be refilled periodically with water, limiting their range. However, they had a simple engine design, fast acceleration, low pollution, economy, and great power. Although many of the steamer's weaknesses were overcome, they suffered from the limited infusion of capital into their production, some untimely accidents, and, eventually, vigorous competition. Nevertheless, around 1900, of the approximately eight thousand automobiles on the road, most were steam-driven.

Rise of the Electrics

Robert Anderson, a British inventor, developed the first crude electric vehicle in the 1830s, but it wasn't until the second half of the nineteenth century that French and English inventors built some of the first practical electric cars. The Flocken Elektrowagen, built in 1888 by German Andreas Flocken, is regarded as the first real electric car of the world. In the United States, the first successful electric car made its debut around 1890, thanks to William Morrison, a chemist who lived in Des Moines, Iowa. His six-passenger vehicle, capable of a top speed of fourteen miles per hour, was little more than an electrified wagon, but it helped spark interest in electric vehicles.

Over the next few years, electric vehicles from various automakers began popping up across America. New York City had a fleet of more than sixty electric taxis. By 1900, electric cars were at their heyday, accounting for around a third of all vehicles on the road, and during the next ten years, they continued to show strong sales. As a road vehicle, though, electric cars had a major problem: limited range. At the turn of the twentieth century, they could only go twenty miles before requiring a recharge.

However, electric cars did have advantages to cars powered by steam or gasoline. They were quiet, easy to drive, and didn't emit a smelly pollutant. They became popular with urban residents—especially women. They were perfect for short trips around the city, and poor road conditions outside cities meant few cars of any type could venture farther. As more people in cities gained access to electricity in the 1910s, it became easier to charge electric cars, adding to their popularity with drivers from all walks of life (including some of the "best known and prominent makers of gasoline cars," as a 1911 *New York Times* article pointed out). Thomas Edison thought electric vehicles were the superior technology and worked to build a better electric vehicle battery.

However, other developments contributed to the decline of the electric vehicle. By the 1920s, the United States had a better system of roads connecting cities, and Americans wanted to get out and explore. Very few Americans outside of cities had electricity at that time, so recharging ranged from difficult to impossible. Also, with the discovery of crude oil in Texas, gas became cheap and readily available for rural Americans, and filling stations began popping up across the country. For these reasons, as well as the introduction of the gasoline-powered Model T, electric vehicles had all but disappeared by 1935.

The Internal Combustion Engine

The first gasoline-fueled, four-stroke cycle engine was built in Germany in 1876. In 1886, Carl Benz began the first commercial production of motor vehicles with internal combustion engines. By the 1890s, motorcars reached their modern stage of development. In fact, the models of that decade were so successful that there has been no fundamental change in the principles of the ordinary auto-mobile engine since that time.

While gasoline cars had promise, they weren't without their faults. They required a lot of manual effort to drive—changing gears was no easy task, and the vehicles needed to be started with a hand crank, making them difficult for some to operate. (The electric starter provided impetus to the eventual acceptance of gasoline-powered cars.) They were also noisy, and their exhaust was unpleasant.

Early on, gasoline-fueled vehicles had stiff competition from steam-driven and electric cars. In fact, of the forty-two hundred cars built in the United States in 1900, only one-fourth employed internal combustion engines. The internal combustion engine as a power plant was enhanced by the increasing availability of gasoline and favorable publicity from automobile race results. In 1900, Ransom E. Olds, a prominent manufacturer of the time, switched from producing steam-driven cars to producing gasoline-fueled vehicles, and in 1903, Henry Ford founded a motorcar company specializing in automobiles with internal combustion engines. It sold seventeen hundred cars in its first full year of business.

Production of automobiles progressed smartly in the very early twentieth century. Besides the German and American manufacturers, cars were built with varying degrees of success in France, Belgium, Switzerland, Sweden, Denmark, Norway, Italy, and even Australia. Mass production began in both France and the United States.

Introduced in 1908, it was Ford's Model T that eventually destroyed the market for steam and electric-powered cars in the early twentieth century. When Ford went to mass production of the Model T, he brought to the market a vehicle that was modestly priced, easy to maintain, relatively fast and powerful, able to travel long distances, and fueled by a cheap, abundant, widely available source of energy. It cost less than half the price of an equivalent electric car. He also paid his workers enough to be able to purchase the cars they were man-ufacturing. This helped push wages and auto sales upward. With the advent of the Model T, the car ceased to be a toy for the rich and firmly entrenched the internal combustion vehicle as the standard. By 1920, Ford had sold over a million cars.

A historian has said that Henry Ford freed common people from the limita-tions of their geography. The automobile created mobility on a scale never known before, and the total effect on living habits and social customs is endless. The convenience of the automobile freed people from the need to live near rail lines or stations. It radically changed city life by accelerating the outward expansion of population into the suburbs. Motor vehicles and paved roads narrowed the gap between rural and urban life. Farmers could ship easily and economically by truck and could drive to larger towns and cities when convenient. Institutions such as regional schools and hospitals became accessible by bus and car.

As a result, demand for gasoline was the major impetus for the growth of the petroleum industry in the twentieth century. By 1973 transportation was responsible for more than half of all consumption of petroleum in the United States, and by 1990 for almost 64 percent. Gasoline consumption soared from less than three billion gallons in 1919 to approximately 15 billion in 1929, 46.5 billion in 1955, and more than 135 billion in 2002. Today, internal combustion engines are responsible for about 90 percent of the energy consumed for travel in the United States.

Later Automotive Development

There were some important developments in the 1960s and 1970s. The market changed as the US "Big Three" automakers—Ford, Chevy, and Chrysler—began facing competition from imported cars. European automakers adopted advanced technologies, and Japan emerged as a car-producing nation. Requirements for stricter automobile emissions and safety increased. Smaller-sized cars grew in popularity.

Uneven oil prices and gasoline shortages—peaking with the 1973 Arab Oil Embargo—created a growing interest in lowering the US dependence on foreign oil and finding homegrown sources of fuel. Congress took note and passed the Electric and Hybrid Vehicle Research, Development, and Demonstration Act of 1976, authorizing research and development in electric and hybrid vehicles.

Around this same time, many big and small automakers began exploring options for alternative fuel vehicles, including electric cars. For example, General Motors developed a prototype for an urban electric car that it displayed at the Environmental Protection Agency's First Symposium on Low Pollution Power Systems Development in 1973, and the American Motor Company produced electric delivery jeeps that the United States Postal Service used in a 1975 test program. Even NASA helped raise the profile of the electric vehicle when its electric lunar rover became the first manned vehicle to drive on the moon in 1971.

Yet the alternative-fueled vehicles developed and produced in the 1970s still suffered from drawbacks compared to gasoline-powered cars. Electric vehicles during this time still had limited performance—usually topping out at speeds of forty-five miles per hour—and their typical range was limited to forty miles before needing to be recharged. Technology in electric vehicles and other alternative-fueled vehicles was essentially stagnant for the entire twentieth century. This began to change dramatically in the twenty-first century.

Notes

1. A rentier state is one in which the state secures tremendous amounts of revenue from the sale of a natural resource, often oil. Because the high revenues come from the sale of natural resources and not taxation, citizens of rentier states are able to enjoy high

standards of living but limited opportunities for political participation. Rentier states are not accountable to their citizens in the ways that governments funded by taxation are. As a result, the exchange that is made between a rentier state and its citizens is material wealth for political consent.

2. Stephen McGlinchey, review of *American Ascendance, British Retreat, and the Rise of Iran in the Persian Gulf* by W. Taylor Fain, *E-International Relations*, November 15, 2010. https://www.e-ir.info/2010/11/15/american-ascendance-british-retreat-and-the-rise-of-iran -in-the-persian-gulf/.

3. Kaeli Subberwal, "Echoes of the Cold War: Russia's Role in Syria," *The Gate*, October 25, 2015, http://uchicagogate.com/articles/2015/10/25/echoes-of-the-cold-war-russias-role-in -syria/.

4. Martin Melosi, "Energy Use and the Internal Combustion Engine," on *The Automobile and the Environment in American History* (website), accessed August 1, 2018, http://www .autolife.umd.umich.edu/Environment/E_Overview/E_Overview2.htm.

5 What Is the Technology Today—and What Does the Future Hold?

ONE OF THE best trends in automotive technology is that the general media is following so many of the new developments. Great credit goes to Elon Musk of Tesla, who not only has great media skills but also a very expansive vision for the future of transportation. In the midst of incremental movement by many carmakers, Musk has upped the stakes for everybody. Clearly passionate about changing the power source of transportation, he also is sharing all of his automotive patents with the world.

Elon Musk has been vocal about his reasons for adopting electric vehicles. It is interesting that Marc Tarpenning, one of the founders of Tesla, was quoted in 2013 (in the book *Tesla Motors: How Elon Musk and Company Made Electric Cars Cool and Sparked the Next Tech Revolution*) as saying, "I worked in the Middle East for years and the idea of sending all of our treasure to the Middle East just doesn't appeal to me."

There are competing technologies for alternative transportation energy, including fuel cells, natural gas, propane, and electricity. However, for passenger travel and light trucks, it appears that electricity will become more prominent more quickly. James Woolsey, former director of the Central Intelligence Agency, when referring to plug-in technology, said, "We must encourage the commercialization of technologies that are compatible with existing infrastructure . . . we don't need a Manhattan Project to make this happen." So for now, let's turn our attention to electric vehicles.

But before we can discuss electric transportation, it is important to understand the basic concept of a kilowatt-hour. The cost of a purely electric car or a plug-in hybrid very much depends on the kilowatt-hour cost of the battery in the car.

A kilowatt-hour (kWh) is a unit of energy that is equivalent to one kilowatt (1 kW) of power sustained for one hour. For instance, an electric heater rated at one thousand watts (1 kW) operating for one hour uses one kilowatt-hour of energy. A television rated at one hundred watts operating for ten hours continuously uses one kilowatt-hour. A forty-watt light bulb operating continuously for twenty-five hours uses one kilowatt-hour.

The chart in figure 5.1, from the Department of Energy, clearly shows the rapid drop in the cost of kilowatt-hours in plug-in vehicles in recent years. Since electric cars are now cost-competitive or nearly cost-competitive based on a

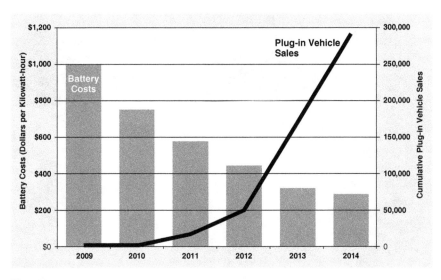

Figure 5.1.

total-cost-of-ownership model, then the continued drop in the cost of the battery, the primary variable cost of an electric car, is significant.

The chart stops at 2014 but the overall trend is still valid today. (An exception would be in 2015, as the result of a comprehensive redesign process for two of the most prominent vehicles in the marketplace, the Chevy Volt and the Nissan Leaf, when buyers were waiting for the updated models.)

It is noteworthy that plug-in electrics (plug-in hybrids and all-electrics are referred to by the acronym "PEV") reached one million in worldwide sales by September of 2015. This was achieved in four years and ten months, which is almost twice as fast as it took regular hybrid sales to achieve the same milestone (just over nine years).

It also has become clear that almost all of the German automakers are moving in this direction, along with the Japanese and American automakers. The years 2019–22 will see the introduction of dozens of new plug-in hybrid and all-electric models from around the world.

Types of Vehicles

It is important to understand the terminology and technology being sold today. There are numerous variations as manufacturers try to differentiate themselves, but the basics are very similar.

Hybrid Electric Vehicles or Hybrids (HEVs)

HEVs are powered by an internal combustion engine and an electric motor that uses energy stored in a battery. HEVs run on gasoline and cannot be plugged in like

Figure 5.2. Toyota Prius hybrid. Source: Author

an all-electric or plug-in hybrid vehicle. The battery is charged primarily through regenerative braking, which allows the battery to capture energy normally lost through braking. The extra power provided by the electric motor allows for a smaller engine, resulting in better fuel economy without sacrificing performance. As a result, HEVs are more fuel-efficient than comparable conventional vehicles.

Driving a hybrid is essentially driving a normal internal combustion engine car with comparable power and better fuel efficiency. You are not driving miles on electricity. I can remember when a friend of mine told me recently that he had bought a hybrid sedan, which he thought was a radical notion, and that he loved it. He didn't know that a hybrid car was perfectly in the mainstream already, and hardly a wild idea. He was behind the times a bit. I just shook my head.

While I appreciate the advances in technology, I don't believe hybrids are anywhere close to sufficient in addressing national security concerns. There is some downward movement on oil use thanks to better fuel efficiency, but that does not fundamentally alter the fact that the worldwide use of oil is a grave national security concern that drains human and financial resources from our country. Hybrids don't move the strategic needle. Running most miles on electricity is a much better choice.

Remember the picture of the mileage on my 2017 Volt (figure 5.4)? You can see that the overall efficiency is well over two hundred miles per gallon. That sort of efficiency—available right now—would have a dramatic impact on national security if all light vehicles worldwide performed likewise.

Figure 5.3. Ford Fusion hybrid (police). Source: Erik Nelsen / NREL

Figure 5.4.

Plug-In Hybrid Electric Vehicles (PHEV)

Plug-in hybrid electric vehicles (PHEVs) use a battery to power an electric motor and also use another fuel, such as gasoline, for power when needed. There is usually a short range for pure electric miles that varies from around twenty miles for some models to fifty-three miles for the current model of the Chevy Volt. This takes advantage of the lower cost of electric miles while providing the security of an internal combustion engine for range and refueling. In a PHEV, you do not have to run on electricity ever, but in the vast majority of circumstances, electric miles are much cheaper. For instance, in the Midwest, I usually talk in terms of one hundred miles. I round off the numbers because they can vary depending on the current price of gasoline, but I tell people that traveling one hundred miles on gasoline may cost you about fifteen dollars. To travel one hundred miles on electricity can cost you less than two dollars.

The initial cost of a PHEV is usually higher than a comparable non-PHEV, but depending on your driving needs, the total cost of ownership may be much less with a PHEV. Looking again at the Department of Energy chart above, you can see that if the cost per kilowatt-hour continues to decrease, even the initial cost may be comparable or lower in a few years. The technology is moving rapidly. Additionally, there are still federal tax credits available to PHEV buyers, and some states have additional tax credits available too.

Plug-in hybrids are a perfect "bridge technology" between internal combustion engines today and all-electric or otherwise alternatively fueled cars in the near future. If the number of all-electric miles on the car is around fifty miles, most drivers would never use gasoline except on longer trips. The total range for most of these vehicles, using a combination of electric and gas, is over 350 miles. There is no range anxiety, ever.

Most of the PHEVs on the market are sedans and small SUVs, but now Chrysler has entered the market with the Pacifica, the first plug-in hybrid, family-size minivan. This is an important development, but interestingly, Chrysler is marketing it as a regular hybrid even though it has thirty to forty miles of pure electric miles before the gasoline engine takes over. That means taking the kids to school, practices, concerts, or whatever will use mostly, if not all, electric miles on a daily basis. However, the minivan can take long trips easily because it has the gasoline engine when needed, just like a regular minivan.

Instruments inside some electric cars have options for the techies, but the instruments inside the Pacifica are set up like a normal minivan, with some simple energy gauges in case the driver wants to monitor them. Most people don't. On May 7, 2017, Sam Abuelsamid observed in *Forbes*, "The core idea here is that busy parents that are hauling multiple kids around don't have time for this nonsense. They just want to get in and drive and not worry about getting all the settings right for maximum efficiency. Thus, the only thing the Pacifica

Figure 5.5. Chevy Volt plug-in hybrid. Source: Author

Figure 5.6. Toyota Prius plug-in hybrid. Source: George Beard / NREL

Figure 5.7. Chrysler Pacifica minivan plug-in hybrid. Source: Simon Edelman / US DOE

hybrid driver needs to do is plug the van in when they come home at night and unplug it in the morning. No muss, no fuss." Frankly, that's what I do with my Volt.

Despite such impressive advances, there is much misinformation regarding these vehicles. Many people still believe that there is some sort of transition while driving that occurs when the power converts from electricity to gasoline. But in fact, when driving these vehicles, you will notice absolutely no difference in the car or its performance; it just keeps going. You won't know that it has converted to gasoline unless you look at the gauges or monitors in the car.

There is also much misinformation regarding charging at home. Many people believe that you must buy equipment to charge the car at home, but actually, it is optional.

For my first five years as mayor of Indianapolis, GM provided Corvettes or Camaros as Indianapolis 500 pace cars to many individuals in the city as a marketing tool. Because of our initiatives in the city, in 2013, GM asked if I wanted a Volt instead. Of course I said, "Yes." I frequently joked that I had the only plug-in hybrid pace car in the world. At the time, the Volt got thirty-eight miles on electricity before converting to gasoline.

I'll explain charging in more detail soon, but suffice it to say that it took three seconds to plug in the Volt in my garage into a normal wall socket (known as Level 1). It would charge fully overnight. You can use Level 2 charging at home also, which is equivalent to the line that runs the dryer in your home. That will

Figure 5.8. Tesla Model S EV. Source: Author

normally include additional equipment to charge the car. The main benefit of Level 2 charging is that it goes four or five times faster than Level 1. Most utilities will help you set up this level of charging.

All-Electric Vehicles (EV or BEV)

EVs are powered by a battery that is charged by plugging it in. There is no other power source. These vehicles require much less maintenance, are very quiet, and have a low cost of operation. Some Tesla models get over 250 miles on a full charge, but most of the newest EVs get between 200 and 250 miles. Range anxiety occurs only on long trips, not in daily use.

Almost all manufacturers today are looking at all-electric cars that will have over two hundred miles of range. The Tesla Model 3, the Chevy Bolt, and the soon-to-be remodeled Nissan Leaf will all have at least two hundred miles of range. Local and regional travel will not be an issue. However, the time to recharge EVs on longer trips is a concern, but many manufacturers are predicting even greater range in the very near future, and with electricity being ubiquitous and the increasing infrastructure for EVs, there is potential for great change. If the federal government and state governments can assist, the change would come much more quickly.

Figure 5.9. Chevy Bolt. Source: Author

Other Power Sources

There are other alternative power sources emerging in transportation, but none yet have electricity's potential in the near future to replace the use of oil.

Fuel cell (FCEV)—An FCEV uses hydrogen as a fuel. A fuel cell combines hydrogen gas with air to produce electricity, which in turn drives an electric motor. Similar to internal combustion engines, FCEVs can have a range of over three hundred miles and can be refueled in less than five minutes. FCEVs are in their very first stages of development, and few car manufacturers make them currently, but Honda and Toyota already have made substantial investments in the technology.

Fueling infrastructure is a huge problem for FCEVs. There are a few fueling stations in California and almost none elsewhere.

Propane and compressed natural gas (CNG)—Propane and CNG act much like gasoline-powered engines and often are used in fleets of buses or trucks. Many school buses are powered by propane. Sometimes larger trucks use either CNG or liquefied natural gas (LNG). Cummins, perhaps the most-respected truck engine manufacturer in the world, makes a superior natural gas engine. Adoption of that engine would be expedited if the refueling infrastructure, which

Figure 5.10. Toyota Mirai fuel cell. Source: iStock

Figure 5.11. Honda Clarity fuel cell. Source: iStock

Figure 5.12. Propane bus being fueled. Source: Dennis Schroeder / NREL

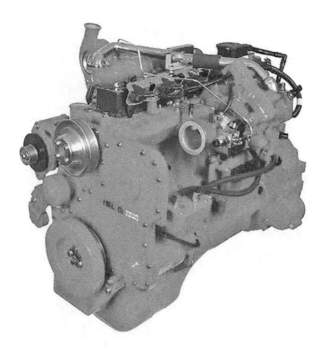

Figure 5.13. Cummins natural gas engine

is growing smartly, would become a priority for federal and state governments. Supply of natural gas is not an issue at all; it is plentiful, and the United States has more natural gas than any nation in the world.

Levels of Charging

As explained on the website evtown.org, from which much of the following information is derived, electric vehicle charging equipment is commonly categorized into one of the three types described below. Environmental factors, particularly cold weather, can affect charging time (as well as driving time). However, this effect is sometimes exaggerated.

Level 1 Charging

Level 1 equipment provides charging through a 120-volt, alternating-current (AC) plug and requires a dedicated circuit. Generally speaking, Level 1 charging refers simply to the use of a standard household outlet.

Level 1 charging equipment is standard on plug-in vehicles; therefore it is portable and does not require installation of any charging equipment. On one end of the cord provided is a standard, three-prong household plug. On the other end is a connector, which plugs into the vehicle. The length of time required to recharge a battery varies with the size of the battery. The most common place for Level 1 charging is at the vehicle owner's home, and the charging is typically conducted overnight.

Level 2 Charging

Level 2 equipment offers charging through a 240V AC plug and requires installation of home charging or public charging equipment. These units require a dedicated circuit.

Level 2 charging equipment is compatible with all electric vehicles and plug-in electric hybrid vehicles. A Level 2 charger has a cord that plugs directly into the vehicle in the same connector location used for Level 1 equipment. Level 2 chargers are commonly found in residential settings, public parking areas, places of employment, and commercial settings. The chargers that one sees in malls or along the street are usually Level 2 chargers. I believe that chargers will eventually show up at places like restaurants to attract customers.

Level 3 Charging

Although this is the fastest charge available, there is currently no industry standard for this level of charging. For instance, Tesla has a proprietary Level 3 Supercharger. There is also a technology called CHAdeMO, commonly known as DC fast charging.

Although not as fast as filling up at a gas station, this technology continues to improve. Most electric cars can receive seventy-five to one hundred miles of charge in half an hour, while Teslas can receive over 150 miles of charge in half an hour. This makes them ideal for restaurants on cross-country trips. These chargers are starting to be deployed across the United States in public and commercial settings.

Adoption of Vehicle Technology

Note these recent headlines:

- "Global Carmakers to Invest At Least $90 Billion in Electric Vehicles"—Reuters, January 15, 2018
- "BMW Unveils Electric-Car Plans for 2021 and Beyond"—*The Globe and Mail*, January 26, 2018
- "Mercedes is About to Unveil an Entire Fleet of Electric Vehicles"—Bloomberg, August 4, 2016
- "Audi Plans to Launch a New Electric Vehicle Model Every Year"—*Fortune*, May 12, 2016
- "Ford Plans $11 Billion Investment, 40 Electrified Vehicles by 2022"—CNBC, January 15, 2018
- "GM Plans to Launch 10 Electric Cars in China by 2020"—ABC News, April 21, 2017
- "Toyota to Introduce 10 Electric Cars by mid-2020s"—CNET, December 18, 2017
- "Honda CEO Shifts Focus to Electric Vehicles"—*Wall Street Journal*, February 2, 2016

Why are all the major manufacturers moving quickly to build electric cars? Because they are aware of these headlines:

- "To Promote Electric Cars, China Considers Move To Ban Gas Guzzlers"—*Forbes*, September 10, 2017
- "India to Sell Only Electric Cars by 2030"—CNN, June 3, 2017
- "Germany To Ban Cars Running On Fuel, All New Cars To Be Made Electric By 2030"—*India Times*, June 17, 2016
- "France Wants to Ban the Sale of All Gas and Diesel Cars By 2040"—*Road and Track*, July 6, 2017
- "Electric Cars Win? Britain to Ban New Petrol and Diesel Cars from 2040"—Reuters, July 26, 2017
- "Norway to 'Completely Ban Petrol Powered Cars by 2025'"—*Independent* (UK), June 4, 2016

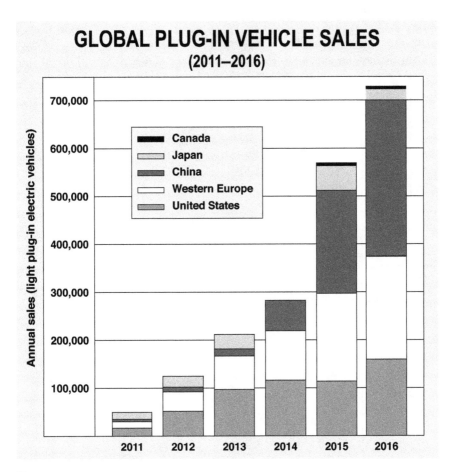

Figure 5.14.

When China, India, France, Germany, and Britain are about to ban the sale of cars with internal combustion engines, the manufacturers have no choice but to adapt.

Adapting is exactly what they are doing. Despite what some may tell you, customers are also adapting. The rate of adoption of these vehicles is relatively rapid, though the numbers are still small when seen as a percentage of the overall car population. Why the rapid growth? More people are realizing these cars are safe, practical, reliable, and now cost-effective for most people. The costs will only continue to decrease as the cost of batteries continues to come down, as indicated in the first chart in this chapter. The accompanying charts, indicating global adoption and US adoption of plug-in electric vehicles, tell a similar tale. The data in these charts are derived from the Department of Energy, the Electric Drive Transportation Association, and Hybridcars.com.

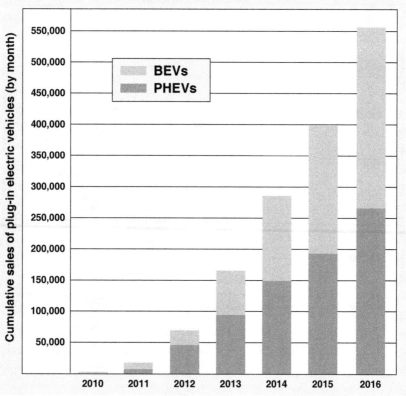

PLUG-IN/EV SALES IN U.S.

by monthly sales of all-electric cars (BEVs) and plug-in hybrids (PHEVs)
(December 2010–December 2016)

Figure 5.15.

Examining worldwide adoption by country reveals some interesting patterns. The numbers in table 5.1 are derived from Hybridcars.com and EVSales.com.

The United States was in the top 10 for "Market Share New Car Sales" in 2013 and 2014 but has dropped back as other countries have moved more aggressively toward the electric car market. The US adoption rate seems to be more of a slow, steady march, versus a more sudden ramp-up in interest as a result of the generous incentives sometimes offered by other nations. Note that if California is considered separately, the 2016 figure for electric car sales there is estimated at 3.5 percent, which would be fourth-best in the world.

Many countries have a buying pattern like China's (see figure 5.16), which now is the world's largest car market. The Chinese have several companies selling

Table 5.1: Electric Car Market Share of Total New Car
Sales in 2016

Top Ten Countries	
Country	**Market Share**
Norway	29.1%
Netherlands	6.4%
Iceland	4.6%
Sweden	3.5%
Switzerland	1.8%
Belgium	1.8%
Austria	1.6%
France	1.4%
United Kingdom	1.4%
China	1.3%

electric cars, and the vast majority of them are made by Chinese car manufacturers. Data is primarily from China Association of Automobile Manufacturers.

More evidence of the rapidly growing acceptance of these technologies is the racing series called Formula E (figure 5.17). It races worldwide in such places as London, Paris, Montreal, and Beijing. In the United States, these vehicles have raced in Long Beach, California, and New York City. The top speed is about 140 mph.

Lithium

Lithium is the main component of the batteries that power electric cars. As such, the security of that mineral is critical. Lithium is produced mainly in Chile, Argentina, Bolivia, Australia, China, and the United States. There is no issue with the quantities available for the foreseeable future if electric cars are adopted at the current rate. Far in to the future (several decades), supply could become an issue, but again, the technology will continue to get better and there are substitutes for lithium if needed. No one is credibly worried about the supply of lithium. Bringing our troops home from guarding the oil infrastructure around the world is a much more pressing issue.

Oil Subsidies

Much is made of the subsidies and incentives for alternative-fueled vehicles in the United States. A quick search of the Internet on the Chevy Volt would refer you to articles from 2011–12, claiming that, because the federal government and some state incentives provided a total of $3 billion to help develop the Volt, that each Volt sold actually cost the taxpayer $250,000. Someone just mentioned this figure to me recently, in fact, while trying to explain how these cars are heavily subsidized by everyone else. Of course, many more Volts have been sold since

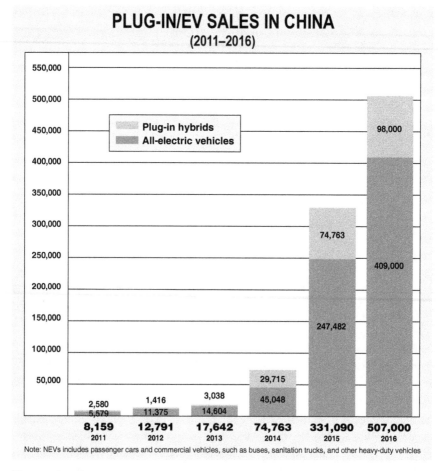

Figure 5.16.

then (so that $250,000 is now well below $30,000 and quickly dropping). The fact that the readily available technology—if it were adopted worldwide or even just nationally—would have a major positive impact on our national security, is ignored.

And as with most arguments, there is another side to the story. There is no question that oil, too, has been subsidized, and for decades. In the documentary *The Burden*, Vice Admiral (retired) and assistant secretary of the Navy Dennis McGinn mentions that if gas were $3.50 per gallon at the pump, then the real cost of that gallon of gas would actually be about $7 or $8 per gallon, because of the costs of our deployed troops defending the flow of oil. He says, "We are paying it; we're just not paying it at the pump." Think about that the next time you fill up.

Figure 5.17. Formula E racing. Source: Alamy

Oil companies also are subsidized in the ways other companies are. Subsidies for exploration and production are common and even the manufacturer's tax deduction, passed in 2004 in response to China's rise in manufacturing, was extended to oil companies.

In his book *Powering Forward*, former Colorado governor Bill Ritter explains how the Department of Interior leases federal land to companies that produce oil and other commodities. In 2008, the Government Accountability Office (GAO) found that the Department of Interior had not evaluated these lease arrangements in more than twenty-five years, ensuring they are below market rates. Five years later, in 2013, the Department of Interior still hadn't evaluated its royalty rates, effectively giving another subsidy for the production of oil.

As a former municipal executive, I understand the occasional need for incentives to increase employment or to keep a business in place when others are incentivizing them to move. Whether the current mix of incentives is appropriate is almost moot, since Congress won't act on them anytime in the near future. But let's not kid ourselves. At a minimum, this equates to several tens of billions of dollars per year, making the largely one-time Chevy Volt incentive look puny by comparison.

Of even greater consequence, as I have explained, is the cost of protecting the oil infrastructure around the world—a cost estimated to be about $70 billion annually. We should also add in the trillions of dollars spent for wars and other conflicts in the Middle East over the last forty years, as well as the enormous loss of human life. All this for protecting a commodity: oil. There are now alternatives available for that commodity.

It is time to pursue these alternatives and bring our troops home from the Middle East.

Substitute Goods

In economic theory, there is the concept of substitute goods. Substitute goods are two goods that can be used for the same purpose. For instance, Pepsi and Coke are substitute goods. The concept is that if the price of one good increases, then the demand for the substitute good is likely to rise. If Coke increases the price of its product, then demand will decrease for Coke, while the demand for Pepsi will increase. It is a simple concept that is largely true.

As I've mentioned before, OPEC and others control the supply of oil to their benefit, not to ours. Oil-dependent nations are at a disadvantage that is almost impossible to overcome given the current transportation technology. If there were a competitive substitute, then that advantage could swing to the currently oil-dependent nations.

Admittedly, substituting transportation technology is not as simple as substituting Pepsi for Coke. It is interesting, though, that when new technologies arise in transportation technology, one of two things happens.

The first is a concerted effort to eliminate that technology. Examples of this include the case of GM's EV1, which was removed from the market, as shown in the 2006 documentary *Who Killed the Electric Car?*—along with the negative press and the spread of misinformation regarding the recent improvements in electric vehicles.

The second is that the price of oil is manipulated—that is, lowered—in an attempt to discourage people from moving away from internal combustion engines. Even as the United States finds more oil, OPEC continues to add to the supply, thereby keeping the price for gasoline low. I'm all for cheap energy, but there has been manipulation of the price of oil for decades, and it is our troops and taxpayers who pay that burden.

The charts in this chapter that relate to the pace at which consumers are adopting electric vehicles are scary to oil producers, and they are reacting. But consider Vice Admiral McGinn's analysis (suggesting that the gas that costs $3.50 per gallon at the pump actually costs between $7 or $8 per gallon as a result of the deployment of our troops to protect the oil infrastructure) versus the stable, low cost of electricity. Once the public knows this, it is a real incentive to move to the new transportation technology.

6 What Would Happen?

A SEDAN OR SUV with a range of four hundred electric miles and fully rechargeable in five to ten minutes would change the world. That is the range of "convenience" and the speed of a "fill-up" that would make the average person completely comfortable with electric vehicles. Adoption of such a vehicle around the world would bring our troops home from the Middle East and bankrupt the terrorists and those who fund them. The United States would no longer have to protect the oil infrastructure that allows trade throughout the world.

Senator Lugar has said, "We have made choices, as a society, which have given oil a near monopoly on American transportation. Now we must make a different choice in the interest of American national security and our economic future." I agree.

Even if every sedan or light truck/SUV was a plug-in hybrid that gets forty to fifty miles on electricity before converting to gasoline usage (like a Chevy Volt), that would have a significant impact. In the United States, as the charts from a 2009 National Household Travel Survey (authored by the Federal Highway Administration) indicate, most miles driven are local, with the average being just twenty-nine miles per day. Amazingly, over 60 percent of trips are less than six miles. Even rural drivers average less than forty miles per day. SAFE estimates we would save about half of our oil usage if only 50 percent of the sedans/light trucks/SUVs in our country had a fifty-mile electric range before converting to gas.

This plug-in hybrid technology is available *right now*. Going forward, there is no excuse to not have this technology on every light vehicle.

Since sedans and light trucks/SUVs account for about 90 percent of highway miles driven, according to the US Department of Transportation, there would be the added convenience of allowing a large number of drivers to recharge at home, most likely at a slower but cheaper rate. Also, and perhaps most important, electricity is ubiquitous—much more so than gas stations. Level 2 charging stations would become an attraction for customers so that "fill-ups" would more than likely occur at malls, restaurants, movie theaters, and work.

Unless Level 3 charging becomes the norm, fueling your car would not be a separate activity as it is now with gas stations; charging your car could be just part of your day at work, at the store, at home—wherever you are.

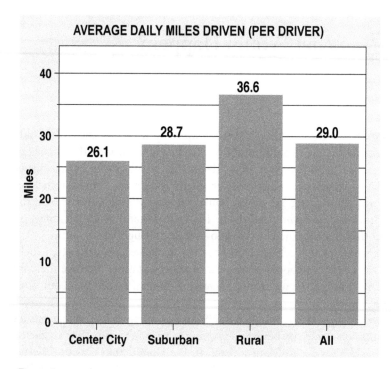

Figure 6.1.

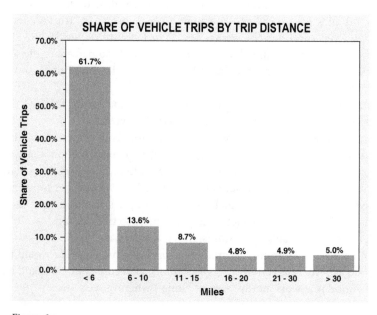

Figure 6.2.

The convenience and conversion that could happen in the United States and Europe would be much more difficult, however, in many parts of Asia. The United States could use its technological advantage to help these countries convert to transportation technology that doesn't fund our nation's enemies. It comes down to whether we want to keep our troops protecting the worldwide oil infrastructure and prolonging a deadly forty-year struggle, or whether we want to help China and India advance their transportation technology so that we can bring our troops home and save American lives and treasure. To me, that's not a close call.

Disruption

A change of this magnitude would cause disruption in several areas—some beneficial, some not so much. In any case, since most people keep their cars for many years, the transition, when moving fully in the proper direction, would take ten to twenty years.

I am anything but an isolationist, but the first two disruptions discussed next—strategic leverage and flow of money—would be of major benefit to the United States and its allies.

Strategic Leverage

The most important change would be a major shift in strategic leverage. Oil-exporting countries could no longer outmaneuver oil-dependent nations. The relationship between Russia and Europe would change. OPEC would hold no strategic weight whatsoever. We could negotiate with these countries or not, but we would not have to do so with the thought of energy resources being withheld if there is disagreement (like the oil embargoes of the 1970s). All those presidential proclamations quoted in the first chapter could come true.

Flow of Money

The dollars flowing from North America, Europe, and Asia to the Middle East and Russia would drop precipitously. That money could be used for more local economic activities instead of being transferred to, in Senator Lugar's words, "some of the least accountable regimes in the world." Europe in particular would benefit by not having to import over of a third of its oil-based energy from Russia.

National Economies

There is no question that a number of economies would weaken. Because the percentage of government revenue derived from oil is very high in several countries, such a shift may result in social unrest. (To its credit, Saudi Arabia has already mentioned plans for a post-oil economy; see Appendix C.) Since the potential transition would occur over ten or twenty years, there would be time to plan. Again, the United States could help in this transition, as could Europe. Social unrest, particularly in the Middle East, has been difficult to manage even with the flow of money heading that way. It would be worse if the oil money were to dry up slowly with no prior planning for a post-oil economy.

The Oil Industry

There is also no question that the oil industry would be reduced. However, even after a long transition period, oil would continue to be used for many everyday products. Most people know that oil and its byproducts are used in such materials as plastics, waxes, and asphalt, but it is also used for chewing gum, lipstick, toothpaste, guitar strings, and a continuing wide range of products. The industry won't go away, but it will not be a strategic necessity as it is now.

Industries always come and go. When the automobile became mass-produced, a whole host of industries went by the wayside. (You don't see many horse carriage businesses anymore.) New technologies and new jobs are produced, old technologies and some jobs move aside. It's the nature of advanced economies. We should not resist it, especially since it is our troops who are now paying the highest price. But we should help those individuals who are most affected.

Car Manufacturers/Dealers

First, car manufacturers and dealers would have to learn how to sell these new vehicles. Right now, a common complaint is that the salespeople in dealerships have no interest or incentive to sell these vehicles, and with few exceptions, a trip to almost any dealer would confirm this.

More problematic is that dealers make a significant part of their income from repair work. On electric or fuel cell cars, there is not much repair work to be done. There are hundreds of moving parts on an internal combustion engine, but very few on an electric vehicle. It's only a small exaggeration to say that, on a purely electric car, ensuring the tires are at the correct pressure and the windshield washer fluid is full is about all that is required for service.

Gas Stations

If Level 3 charging for electrics becomes the norm, or if fuel cells predominate, then gas stations could survive. However, I would surmise that most charging for electrics would be at home, malls, the workplace, and retail outlets.

The Electrical Grid

One of the early misconceptions about electric cars was that the grid could not handle them. Not to worry. Even though we are still in a very early stage of adoption, utilities understand the issue and are not worried; remember, they want to sell more electricity. For those who use Level 1 charging (a normal 120V wall socket), there is no issue whatsoever because the increased load at this level of charging can easily be absorbed. The fast Level 3 chargers are usually connected to a commercial-level feed that also can absorb the load. The dedicated Level 2 charger could be an issue if enough electric vehicles were concentrated in a particular neighborhood or area that is dependent on a distributed feed, but the utilities are aware of this and react accordingly.

Even so, demand on the grid is not much of a concern. Sandy Dechert, referencing a study by Navigant Research, cites examples in California, where most electric vehicles are being sold. Pacific Gas and Electric conducts a "grid service check to ensure the local distribution transformer has enough power." Out of ten thousand checks, there were only twelve local upgrades. Additionally, Southern California Edison "attributed less than 1 percent of transformer upgrades directly to plug-in vehicles."[1]

A bonus of electric cars could and probably will be the interactivity between the cars and the grid. Charging hours actually could be predetermined to equalize the load throughout the day, and, perhaps more importantly, the stored electricity in cars could prove to be extremely helpful in disasters such as hurricanes.

The Military

Think of where the military has been deployed most of the last forty years. Besides our standing bases around the world (primarily Asia and Europe), the Middle East has been the focus of our military's efforts, and it is also where most of the actual fighting has taken place. Although no one likes to talk about it, the military is tired, particularly since 9/11. In addition to the enormous hard costs of war, the soft costs of our Middle Eastern endeavors (including Veterans Administration claims and loss of productivity) are well over two trillion dollars, according to a Brown University study.[2] There are numerous indicators that many of our veterans are battling depression.

Again, when my fellow troops and I went to the Gulf War in 1990–91, protecting oil as a commodity was critical to our way of life. But now technology has allowed us the opportunity to move away from oil as a necessity. Let's seize that opportunity.

Additional Ramifications

As mentioned in chapter 1, 90 percent of our transportation needs require oil, and transportation accounts for 70 percent of all oil usage in the country. If oil-based fuel (gasoline and diesel) were not being used for transportation—either completely, as in all-electric, or as a plug-in hybrid that would use electricity for the vast majority of the miles driven—we not only would never import oil, but we could also either help or provide the model for other countries to follow. It would scare the hell out of oil-producing nations that now hold us hostage.

There are additional alternative fuel sources, such as fuel cell (hydrogen), that are still in the earlier stages of proving their capability, but currently, battery-powered cars have the most potential. Their capability is finally increasing at a rather rapid rate.

Further advantages include the price of electricity, which has been stable for decades and not subject to the wild price swings that we have seen in the oil market for the past forty years, thanks to world events or the decisions of those who control the supply of oil. It is difficult for businesses and individuals to plan budgets when their energy costs are dependent on nationalized oil companies that open or close the spigot to their advantage. It is not a free market.

Additionally, electricity tends to be much more local in its production, subject to local forces rather than to a global commodity market. Also, the origin of the electricity can come from multiple sources (solar, wind, natural gas, hydro, etc.) rather than just primarily one commodity, as in transportation. Eventually, if electricity becomes a common transportation energy source, then the interactivity with the grid has potential for efficiencies, along with the stored electricity becoming important in the case of a natural disaster, such as a hurricane or tornado.

If electric cars become more common in China, India, and other nations, then their need to buy oil from countries who wish to do us harm will diminish. Admittedly, India will have a more difficult time as a result of the current unreliability of their electrical grid, but the question should be asked: Is it more beneficial for the United States to help India with its electrical grid than to have India buy oil from Iran? China, for its part and despite its relationship with Iran (a relationship that ensures China has continuing access to oil in the short term) can move rather rapidly toward electricity as a transportation fuel, as figure 5.16 in the previous chapter shows.

Weigh this against having troops engaged in the Middle East for forty years. Former Congressman Bob Inglis of South Carolina lost his seat largely for advocating for alternative energy. The documentary *The Burden* gives him the last word.

Referring to oil, Inglis remarks, "Let's say to the Middle East, 'See if you can drink that stuff.'"

Notes

1. Sandy Dechert, "Grid Capacity for Electric Vehicles is Actually Not a Problem, Studies Find," *Clean Technica*, February 3, 2014, https://cleantechnica.com/2014/02/03/grid-capacity-electric-vehicles-actually-problem-studies-find/.

2. Neta C. Crawford, "US spending on post 9/11 wars to reach 5.6 trillion by 2018," (Cost of War study, Watson Institute for International and Public Affair, Brown University, Providence, RI, November 2017).

7   What Should We Do Now?

As I WRITE this in 2018, I believe that every sedan, SUV, and light truck should be a plug-in hybrid with fifty (and preferably eighty to one hundred) electric miles available before the power converts to gasoline. That would have a dramatic effect on the amount of gasoline we use. The technology is available now, and if the vehicles are designed from the ground up, they will provide all of the power and space equivalent to vehicles being built today.

According to SAFE, a sedan/SUV/light truck that had fifty miles of electric range would drive 80 percent of its total miles on electricity and 20 percent using gasoline. Remember that the average driver travels about twenty-nine miles per day, and that even rural drivers drive fewer than forty miles per day. Only on longer trips would gasoline actually be used.

If only 50 percent of sedans, SUVs, and light trucks had fifty miles of electricity available, oil usage would decrease by 48 percent for these vehicles, from 7.7 million barrels per day to 4.0 million barrels per day. That is staggering. What if 100 percent of these vehicles had fifty miles of electricity available? It would send shivers down the spine of our Middle Eastern adversaries. The technology to do this is available today.

Even though the federal government intervenes frequently in private-market activity, I am not one who likes to rely on the federal government to intervene much. However, if manufacturers do not voluntarily move down the path highlighted above, there is a case for the federal government to mandate such initiatives; it already mandates fuel efficiency. It's difficult for me to advocate for this, but the national security aspect should override any other concerns. A level playing field for all of the manufacturers would be easy to create.

Here are some more recommendations for action.

Individuals

- Understand that there is a direct link between national security and the way we fuel our vehicles. We can start to change.
- Be open to the new technology. No one expects you to get rid of your current car immediately and replace it with a plug-in hybrid. The time to start is when you're planning to purchase your next new car. Too many people do not realize that the technology is moving quickly and that many people and organizations are committed to

moving in a new direction. Most likely there is a car being built right now, or at least by the end of 2020, that will fit your driving needs and will cost much less on a total-cost-of-ownership basis than what you drive now. Almost all manufacturers, domestic and foreign, are moving quickly, particularly with plug-in hybrids.

- Realize that the vehicles are high-tech and reliable. The Chevy Volt was the 2011 North American Car of the Year at the North American International Auto Show as determined by American and Canadian automobile writers, based on its "innovation, design, safety, handling, driver satisfaction, and value." It also ranked first for two years in a row (2011 and 2012) for owner satisfaction by *Consumer Reports* magazine. In 2013, the Tesla Model S was the first car ever to be voted unanimously as *Motor Trend*'s Car of the Year. *Consumer Reports* gave the car its highest rating ever. The National Highway Traffic Safety Administration bestowed its highest-ever safety rating on the Model S. These are just a few of the awards it has won. These are not special category awards, but awards that compare cars in the overall marketplace.

- Routinely go to car dealerships and ask about plug-in hybrids or electric vehicles. The salespeople in most dealerships have no clue about these vehicles and are not required to learn anything about them, although there are some exceptions. I continue to be dismayed when I go into dealerships and once again realize that I know ten times more about the car than the salesperson. Dealerships and their staffs will learn if you just go in and ask about these vehicles, only to walk out when they can't field your questions.

Businesses

- Start converting your fleets. Some cities have made a commitment to switch out fleets once they realized that they could save significant money based on prior practices. Businesses could do the same. Some businesses with truck fleets are converting to natural gas on their own and saving money doing it.

- Put in the infrastructure/charging stations that would not only charge up your own vehicles but also send a message to your employees that these cars are solid and reliable, and that you encourage their use. The cost of doing so is much less than people know. (Residential Level 2 chargers are less than $1,000, while most commercial Level 2 chargers are less than $5,000. Several are below $2,000.) Most businesses do not even look at converting because they have never seen these cars and hear only negative, false comments. Once business leaders start driving them, their opinion improves. The federal government has a Workplace Charging Challenge that can help businesses get started.

- Malls, restaurants, stores, and schools should put in charging stations. The cost of the infrastructure is decreasing greatly, and in most areas of the country, electricity would be a negligible expense in attracting customers. Businesses may start drawing in more customers once the owners of the new technology realize they can come to an establishment and fill up their cars. I do believe that for electric cars, the new fill-up locations will be home and retail outlets, not gas stations or their future equivalent. If fuel cells predominate, a system much like today's gas stations could remain.

Automobile Manufacturers and Dealerships

- While mayor of Indianapolis, I was fortunate to talk to many manufacturers, and I believe that they desire to move toward the new technologies. In the short term, this is difficult because of the general public's lack of knowledge or acceptance. It is incumbent on many people, including manufacturers, to increase this knowledge and acceptance of the new technology.
- Continue to develop new technologies that reduce transportation's dependence on oil. It is particularly important to ensure there is a proper profit margin so that dealerships will feel comfortable selling such vehicles.
- Advertise the cars' benefits rather than relying on the early adopters to spread the message.
- Teach your salespeople. This is a common complaint that is well known throughout the industry. No company can sell a product unless the frontline force has the knowledge and believes in the product. This may entail changing sales incentives, which could be difficult in the short term. But greater consumer acceptance of the technology would lead to much better economies of scale in manufacturing—which, in turn, would help the dealerships react accordingly.

Local Government

- Understand that there are turnkey solutions available to convert your fleets. This could take some political will, but there have been enough examples recently that the transition should be easy to explain to all stakeholders.

- Let your citizenry know that transitioning to plug-in hybrids or purely electric cars will save money for the city, and in the process demonstrate that these are great cars for their personal use as well.

State Government

- Convert your fleet. Plug-in hybrids would be beneficial in almost all state agencies.
- Build a charging infrastructure along highways and thorough-fares, which would encourage the sale of the new transportation technology.

Federal Government

- Too many officeholders like to say, "We don't want to pick winners and losers." They are usually referring to subsidies. Considering political history, this statement is comical. However, when government can partner with private industry, great progress can be made. The highway system and space exploration are but two examples. Let our troops and our country win by not having to defend a global oil market at devastating personal expense and great financial cost.
- Convert the federal fleet. The numbers are staggering, and so are the opportunities. According to the General Services Administration, there are more than five hundred thousand passenger vehicles and light trucks in the federal fleet as of 2013. A conversion could begin with the next budget cycle, which would provide impetus for the manufacturers to move forward also.
- Provide funding for building a charging network along highways. This is obvious and would send a signal to citizens that a significant change is underway. It would also help in standardization of the technology.
- If manufacturers do not move quickly enough toward the new technology, consider mandating that sedans, SUVs, and light trucks have a minimum of fifty miles of electricity before conversion to gasoline. (The federal government already mandates fuel mileage.) This will help create a level playing field for manufacturers. Much of the technology is openly available. For instance, Tesla allows anyone to use its technology, and GM has indicated it will share some technology also. A gentle shove from the federal government could be helpful.
- Help other countries in their conversion. India in particular has great potential. Could we strike a deal to help India with its electrical

grid in exchange for the use of electric cars? Again, our troops and federal budget would be the prime beneficiaries.

- Use national security as the way to convert conservatives to the new technology. They should respond to that argument.

Voters

- Ask pertinent questions of your elected officials and candidates for office. In most cases, officeholders have no information whatsoever about emerging technology in any area, not just in transportation. Legislators in particular respond only to what their constituents ask of them. Ask often and in detail. That is the only way they will learn.
- In some cases, these questions need to be asked of individuals or agencies that are not elected.
- Refer to Appendix A, which concerns congressional donations.

8 A Final Thought

WHEN YOU GO out on the weekend to watch ten- or twelve-year-old kids happily playing Little League baseball or soccer, swimming in a meet, or participating in a robotics tournament or any other such activity, please remember that if we continue on our current path, some of those children will be fighting in the Middle East in just another ten years.

Lest anyone think that statement is too somber or overly dramatic, I would remind you that I could have made that statement accurately anytime from the late 1970s on.

That's four decades' worth of children, many of whom found themselves moving from the playground to the battlefield.

Appendix A
Congressional Donations Data

Although the vast majority of oil reserves are controlled from outside the United States, there is still a tremendous amount of money involved in the domestic oil market. Inevitably, there are individuals and corporations in the industry who are protecting their interests.

Donations to the campaigns of elected officials are part of our political system. Although I would never accuse an official of casting a vote strictly in the interest of a campaign contributor (although history has shown clearly that that has happened), I do believe that an industry that contributes across the board holds enormous collective influence over a particular legislative body.

In Colorado governor Bill Ritter's book *Powering Forward*, he quotes Supreme Court Justice Steven Breyer: "Who, after all, can seriously contend that a $100,000 donation does not alter the way one thinks about—and quite possibly votes—on an issue. . . . It's only natural and it happens all too often, that a busy senator with 10 minutes to spare will spend those minutes returning the call of a large soft-money donor rather than the call of any other constituent."

Governor Ritter's book also quotes from an article by Joseph Stiglitz about the savings-and-loan scandal of the 1980s. When Charles Keating was asked by a member of a Congressional committee whether the $1.5 million Keating gave to elected officials had any influence, he replied, "I certainly hope so."

Below are figures from the Center for Responsive Politics, available on its website at opensecrets.org. These are the political contributions of the oil and gas industry in 2014 only, but the figures in other years are similar. For 2014, 395 of 435 congressional representatives and 92 out of 100 senators received contributions from this industry. Although individual officeholders' receipts are readily available on the website, I chose not to include them.

The breadth and depth of the contributions do tell a story. Both political parties are well represented, and there were even more Democratic senators who received contributions than Republicans, which is probably a surprise to some. However, it is clear that Republicans do receive more contributions per candidate.

In my few talks bringing this subject up to elected representatives in Washington, I've been using the phrase "Their eyes glaze over." Still today, there is no appetite for courage on this subject. That has to change.

2014 POLITICAL CONTRIBUTIONS FROM OIL & GAS INDUSTRY

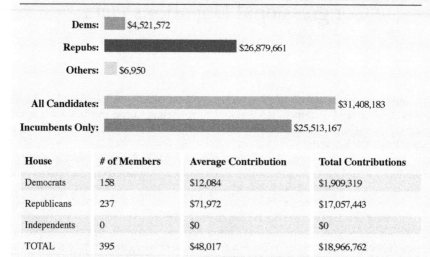

Dems: $4,521,572

Repubs: $26,879,661

Others: $6,950

All Candidates: $31,408,183

Incumbents Only: $25,513,167

House	# of Members	Average Contribution	Total Contributions
Democrats	158	$12,084	$1,909,319
Republicans	237	$71,972	$17,057,443
Independents	0	$0	$0
TOTAL	395	$48,017	$18,966,762

The US House of Representatives has 435 members and 5 non-voting delegates.
Totals may exceed 440 as a result of mid-term replacements.

Senate	# of Members	Average Contribution	Total Contributions
Democrats	47	$45,257	$2,127,120
Republicans	43	$102,411	$4,403,685
Independents	2	$1,500	$3,000
TOTAL	92	$71,020	$6,533,805

The US Senate has 100 members.
Totals may exceed 100 as a result of mid-term replacements.

Figure A.1.

Appendix B
Price of a Barrel of Oil, 1986–2015

The fluctuations in the last fifteen years alone should give one pause, but clearly this is not a free market controlled by the "invisible hand," as described by Adam Smith.

Price Fluctuation of a Barrel of Oil, 1986 to 2015
(July figures from each year)

Year	Price	Year	Price
1986	11.18	2001	26.02
1987	20.92	2002	26.79
1988	15.11	2003	30.08
1989	20.55	2004	39.56
1990	16.94	2005	59.71
1991	20.78	2006	75.20
1992	21.87	2007	71.11
1993	18.29	2008	141.38
1994	19.62	2009	64.06
1995	17.33	2010	71.96
1996	21.48	2011	96.92
1997	19.53	2012	83.72
1998	13.87	2013	97.94
1999	19.78	2014	104.19
2000	30.76	2015	52.48

Appendix C
Even the Saudis Know

The $2-Trillion Project to Get Saudi Arabia's Economy Off Oil

Eight Unprecedented Hours with "Mr. Everything," Prince Mohammed bin Salman.

Peter Waldman

Early last year, at a royal encampment in the oasis of Rawdat Khuraim, Prince Mohammed bin Salman of Saudi Arabia visited his uncle, King Abdullah, in the monarch's final days before entering a hospital. Unbeknown to anyone outside the House of Saud, the two men, separated in age by 59 years, had a rocky history together. King Abdullah once banned his brash nephew, all of 26 at the time, from setting foot in the Ministry of Defense after rumors reached the royal court that the prince was disruptive and power-hungry. Later, the pair grew close, bound by a shared belief that Saudi Arabia must fundamentally change, or else face ruin in a world that is trying to leave oil behind.

For two years, encouraged by the king, the prince had been quietly planning a major restructuring of Saudi Arabia's government and economy, aiming to fulfill what he calls his generation's "different dreams" for a post carbon future. King Abdullah died shortly after his visit, in January 2015. Prince Mohammed's father, Salman, assumed the throne, named his son the deputy crown prince—second in line—and gave him unprecedented control over the state oil monopoly, the national investment fund, economic policy, and the Ministry of Defense. That's a larger portfolio than that of the crown prince, the only man ahead of him on the succession chart. Effectively, Prince Mohammed is today the power behind the world's most powerful throne. Western diplomats in Riyadh call him Mr. Everything. He's 31 years old.

"From the first 12 hours, decisions were issued," says Prince Mohammed. "In the first 10 days, the entire government was restructured." He spoke for eight hours over two interviews in Riyadh that provide a rare glimpse of the thinking of a new kind of Middle East potentate—one who tries to emulate Steve Jobs, credits video games with sparking ingenuity, and works 16-hour days in a land with no shortage of sinecures.

Last year there was near-panic among the prince's advisers as they discovered Saudi Arabia was burning through its foreign reserves faster than anyone knew, with insolvency only two years away. Plummeting oil revenue had resulted in an almost $200 billion budget shortfall—a preview of a future in which the Saudis' only viable export can no longer pay the bills, whether because of shale oil flooding the market or climate change policies. Historically, the kingdom has relied on the petroleum sector for 90 percent of the state budget, almost all its export earnings, and more than half its gross domestic product.

Reprinted with permission from Bloomberg.

On April 25 the prince is scheduled to unveil his "Vision for the Kingdom of Saudi Arabia," an historic plan encompassing broad economic and social changes. It includes the creation of the world's largest sovereign wealth fund, which will eventually hold more than $2 trillion in assets—enough to buy all of Apple, Google, Microsoft, and Berkshire Hathaway, the world's four largest public companies. The prince plans an IPO that could sell off "less than 5 percent" of Saudi Aramco, the national oil producer, which will be turned into the world's biggest industrial conglomerate. The fund will diversify into nonpetroleum assets, hedging the kingdom's nearly total dependence on oil for revenue. The tectonic moves "will technically make investments the source of Saudi government revenue, not oil," the prince says. "So within 20 years, we will be an economy or state that doesn't depend mainly on oil."

For 80 years oil has underwritten the social compact on which Saudi Arabia operates: absolute rule for the Al Saud family, in exchange for generous spending on its 21 million subjects. Now, Prince Mohammed is dictating a new bargain. He's already reduced massive subsidies for gasoline, electricity, and water. He may impose a value-added tax and levies on luxury goods and sugary drinks. These and other measures are intended to generate $100 billion a year in additional nonoil revenue by 2020. That's not to say the days of Saudi government handouts are over—there are no plans to institute an income tax, and to cushion the blow for those with lower incomes, the prince plans to pay out direct cash subsidies. "We don't want to exert any pressure on them," he says. "We want to exert pressure on wealthy people."

Saudi Arabia can't thrive while curbing the rights of half its population, and the prince has signaled he would support more freedom for women, who can't drive or travel without permission from a male relative. "We believe women have rights in Islam that they've yet to obtain," the prince says. One former senior U.S. military officer who recently met with the prince says the royal told him he's ready to let women drive but is waiting for the right moment to confront the conservative religious establishment, which dominates social and religious life. "He said, 'If women were allowed to ride camels [in the time of the Prophet Muhammad], perhaps we should let them drive cars, the modern-day camels,'" the former officer says.

Separately, Saudi Arabia's religious police have been banned from making random arrests without assistance from other authorities. Attempts to liberalize could jeopardize the deal that the Al Saud family struck with Wahhabi fundamentalists two generations ago, but the sort of industries Prince Mohammed wants to lure to Saudi Arabia are unlikely to come to a country with major strictures on women. Today, no matter how much money there is in Riyadh, bankers and their families would rather stay in Dubai.

Many Saudis, accustomed to watching the levers of power operated carefully by the geriatric descendants of the kingdom's founding monarch, were stunned by Prince Mohammed's lightning consolidation of power last year. The ascendance of a third-generation prince—he's the founder's grandson—was of acute interest to the half of the population that's under 25, particularly among the growing number of urbane, well-educated Saudis who find the restrictions on women an embarrassment. Youth unemployment is about 30 percent.

But supporting reform is one thing, and living it another. Public reaction to the economic reboot has been wary, sometimes angry. This winter, many Saudis took to Twitter, their favored means of uncensored discourse, to vent about a jump of as much as 1,000 percent in water bills and to complain about the prospect of Saudi Aramco, the nation's patrimony, being sold off to finance the investment fantasies of a royal neophyte.

"We've been screaming for alternatives to oil for 46 years, but nothing happened," says Barjas Albarjas, an economic commentator who's critical of selling Aramco shares. "Why are we putting our main source of livelihood at risk? It's as if we're getting a loan from the buyer that we'll have to pay back for the rest of our lives."

Albarjas and other Saudi skeptics believe public investors, leery the state will always have other priorities for Aramco besides maximizing profits, will demand a steep discount to invest in its shares. They also wonder why Saudis should trust unaccountable managers of the sovereign wealth fund to bring in high returns any more than Aramco's executives. The company's size is staggering. It's the world's No. 1 oil producer, with the capacity to pump more than 12 million barrels a day, more than twice as much as any other company, and it's the world's fourth-biggest refiner. Aramco controls the world's second-largest oil reserves, behind Venezuela; but in contrast to that country's expensive-to-tap Orinoco Belt, the oil in Saudi Arabia is cheap and easy to obtain. Aramco is also one of the most secretive companies on earth—there are no official measures of financial performance.

Saudi Arabia's economy will probably expand 1.5 percent in 2016, the slowest pace since the global financial crisis, according to a Bloomberg survey, as government spending—the engine that powers the economy—declines for the first time in more than a decade. The state still employs two-thirds of Saudi workers, while foreigners account for nearly 80 percent of the private-sector payroll. Some past diversification drives in Saudi Arabia have been conspicuous failures. The $10 billion King Abdullah Financial District, for example, begun in 2006, sits largely unleased. A ghostly monorail track snakes through some 70 buildings, including five brand-new glass-and-steel skyscrapers. Some construction workers abandoned the project recently, claiming they hadn't been paid.

"Ultimately, everyone knows what the demographics imply for Saudi Arabia," says Crispin Hawes, a managing director at Teneo Intelligence. "Those demographics don't look any nicer now than they did 10 years ago. Without real fundamental economic reform, it is incredibly difficult to see how the Saudi economy can generate the employment levels it needs."

Prince Mohammed won't go into details about any planned nonoil investments, but he says the gargantuan sovereign fund will team up with private equity firms to eventually invest half its holdings overseas, excluding the Aramco stake, in assets that will produce a steady stream of dividends unmoored from fossil fuels. He knows that many people aren't convinced. "This is why I'm sitting with you today," he says in mid-April. "I want to convince our public of what we are doing, and I want to convince the world."

Prince Mohammed says he's used to resistance, hardened by bureaucratic enemies who once accused him of power-grabbing in front of his father and King Abdullah. He says he studies Winston Churchill and Sun Tzu's The Art of War and will turn adversity to his advantage. It could all read as just another millennial's disruption talk if the prince didn't have a clear path to power or speak so freely in ways that shock the petro-political world order.

The likely future king of Saudi Arabia says he doesn't care if oil prices rise or fall. If they go up, that means more money for nonoil investments, he says. If they go down, Saudi Arabia, as the world's lowest-cost producer, can expand in the growing Asian market. The deputy crown prince is essentially disavowing decades of Saudi oil doctrine as the leader of OPEC. He scuttled a proposed freeze of oil production on April 17 at a suppliers' meeting in Qatar because archrival Iran wouldn't participate. Observers saw it as extremely rare interference by a member of the royal family, which has traditionally given the technocrats at the Petroleum Ministry ample room for maneuver on oil policy. "We don't care about oil prices—$30 or $70, they are all the same to us," he says. "This battle is not my battle."

To interview the deputy crown prince, you don't check in with the receptionist. The perimeter begins at a downtown Riyadh hotel, awaiting the call from the office of palace protocol. The evening of March 30 is spent on standby; the word comes at 8:30 p.m. Three Mercedes-Benzes arrive. Even headed to an interview about thrift, there's no escaping decadence: The cars appear brand-new, with seats wrapped in plastic and safety belts that have never been used.

The caravan heads to the royal compound in Irqah, a cluster of palaces surrounded by high white walls where the king and some of his relatives live, including Prince Mohammed. Armed guards, checkpoints, and metal detectors are all bypassed. No one even checks IDs. In his office, Prince Mohammed wears a plain white gown and nothing on his head, revealing longish dark curls and a receding hairline—an informality that many Saudis would find endearing when official photos were later published online. A marathon discussion and interview begins, with him listening to questions in English and responding immediately in detail in Arabic. He repeatedly corrects his interpreter.

At 12:30 a.m., it's dinnertime. The reporters are joined at the table by the prince's economic team, including the chairman of Aramco; the chief financial regulator; and the head of the sovereign wealth fund. As conversation loosens over the meal, Prince Mohammed asks Mohammed Al-Sheikh, his Harvard-educated financial adviser and a former lawyer at Latham & Watkins and the World Bank, to give an update on Saudi Arabia's fiscal condition.

During the oil boom from 2010 to 2014, Saudi spending went berserk. Prior requirements that the king approve all contracts over 100 million riyals ($26.7 million) got looser and looser—first to 200 million, then to 300 million, then to 500 million, and then, Al-Sheikh says, the government suspended the rule altogether.

A journalist asks: How much was wasted?

Al-Sheikh eyes a running recorder on the table. "Can I turn this off?" he says.

"No, you can say it on record," Prince Mohammed says.

"My best guess," says Al-Sheikh, "is that there was roughly between 80 to 100 billion dollars of inefficient spending" every year, about a quarter of the entire Saudi budget.

Prince Mohammed picks up the questioning: "How close is Saudi Arabia to a financial crisis?"

Today it's much better, Al-Sheikh says. But "if you'd asked me exactly a year ago, I was probably on the verge of having a nervous breakdown." Then he tells a story that no one outside the kingdom's inner sanctum has heard. Last spring, as the International Monetary Fund and others were predicting Saudi Arabia's reserves could stake the country for at least five years of low oil prices, the prince's team discovered the kingdom was rapidly becoming insolvent. At last April's spending levels, Saudi Arabia would have gone "completely broke" within just two years, by early 2017, Al-Sheikh says. To avert calamity, the prince cut the budget by 25 percent, reinstated strict spending controls, tapped the debt markets, and began to develop the VAT and other levies. The burn rate on Saudi Arabia's cash reserves—$30 billion a month through the first half of 2015—began to fall.

Al-Sheikh finishes his fiscally mortifying report. "Thank you," the prince says.

A second interview, on April 14, takes place at King Salman's farmhouse in Diriyah, on the outskirts of Riyadh. When the Mercedes caravan gets snarled in freeway traffic, a call from the front seat produces a police escort out of thin air. The reporters pull into a narrow lane running along a high wall that looks like the mud-brick bulwark of a desert castle. The property, where King Salman and his son have offices, sits atop a small hill in the heart of the Al Sauds' ancestral lands.

This time the prince talks about himself. Growing up, he says, he benefited from two influences: technology and the royal family. His generation was the first on the Internet, the first to play video games, and the first to get its information from screens, he says. "We think in a very different way. Our dreams are different."

His father is an avid reader, and he liked to assign his children one book per week, and then quiz them to see who'd read it. His mother, through her staff, organized daily extracurricular courses and field trips and brought in intellectuals for three-hour discussions. Both parents were taskmasters. Being late to lunch with his father was "a disaster," the prince says. His mother was so strict that "my brothers and I used to think, Why is our mother treating us this way? She would never overlook any of the mistakes we made," he says. Now the prince thinks her punishments made them stronger.

The prince had four older half-brothers he looked up to, he says. One was an astronaut who flew on the space shuttle Discovery, the first Arab and Muslim to reach outer space. Another is the respected deputy oil minister. A third became a university professor with a Ph.D. from Oxford in political science, and the fourth, who died in 2002, founded one of the largest media groups in the Middle East. All of them worked closely with King Fahd because he was their father's full brother, the prince explains, "which allowed us to observe and live" the heady atmosphere of the royal court.

Prince Mohammed saw two possible versions of himself: one who pursued a vision of his own, and one who adapted to the court as it was. "There's a big difference," he says. "The first, he can create Apple. The second can become a successful employee. I had elements that were much more than what Steve Jobs or Mark Zuckerberg or Bill Gates had. If I work according to their methods, what will I create? All of this was in my head when I was young."

In 2007, Prince Mohammed graduated fourth in his class from King Saud University with a bachelor's degree in law. Then the kingdom came knocking. He resisted at first, telling the director of the Bureau of Experts, which serves as the cabinet's legal adviser, that he was off to get married, earn a master's degree overseas, and make his fortune. But his father urged him to give the government a chance, and Prince Mohammed did so for two years, focusing on changing certain corporate laws and regulations that "I had always struggled with." His boss, Essam bin Saeed, says the prince showed a restless intellect and no patience for bureaucracy. "Procedures that used to take two months, he'd ask for them in two days," says Saeed, who now works as a minister of state. "Today, it's one day."

In 2009, King Abdullah refused to approve Prince Mohammed's promotion, in theory to avoid the appearance of nepotism. A bitter Prince Mohammed left and went to work for his father, then governor of Riyadh. He stepped into a viper's nest.

As Prince Mohammed tells it, he tried to streamline procedures to keep his father from drowning in a sea of paperwork, and the old guard rebelled. They accused the young prince of usurping power by cutting off their contact with his father and took their complaints to King Abdullah. In 2011, King Abdullah named Prince Salman defense minister but ordered Prince Mohammed never to set foot inside the ministry.

The prince worried his career was over. "I'm saying to myself, 'I'm in my 20s, I don't know how I fell into more than one trap,'" he says. But given how things have turned out, he's grateful. "It's only by coincidence I started working with my father—all because of King Abdullah's decision not to grant my promotion. God bless his soul, he did me a favor."

The prince resigned his government post and went to work reorganizing his father's foundation, which builds housing, and started his own nonprofit aimed at fostering innovation and leadership among Saudi youth. In 2012 his father became crown prince. Six months later, Prince Mohammed was named his chief of court. Gradually, he worked his way back into King Abdullah's good graces, taking on special assignments for the royal court that called for sharp elbows.

As the prince privately began planning for his father's eventual reign, the king came to him with a huge assignment: Clean up the Ministry of Defense. Its problems had defied solutions for years, the prince says. "I told him, 'Please, I don't want this.' He shouted at me and said, 'You're not to blame. I'm the one to blame—for talking to you.'" The last thing Prince Mohammed wanted at the time was more powerful enemies. The king issued a royal decree naming the prince supervisor of the office of defense minister and member of the cabinet.

He brought in Booz Allen Hamilton and Boston Consulting Group and changed the procedures for weapons procurement, contracting, information technology, and human resources, says Fahad Al-Eissa, director general of the defense minister's office. Previously, the legal department had become "marginalized," which resulted in bad contracts that became "a big source of corruption," Al-Eissa says. The prince strengthened the law department and sent back dozens of contracts for revision. Many weapons purchases had been misconceived and inappropriately vetted, with no clear purpose. "We are the fourth-largest military spender in the world, yet when it comes to the quality of our arms, we are barely in the top 20," Al-Eissa says. So the prince created an office to analyze arms deals.

He also started spending a few days a week at King Abdullah's palace. He tried to push through several new reforms. "It was very difficult to do with the presence of a number of people," he says. "But I remember to this day there's nothing I discussed with King Abdullah that he didn't give the order and implement."

Less than a week after King Abdullah died and King Salman took the throne, he issued a decree naming Prince Mohammed defense minister, chief of the royal court, and president of a newly created council to oversee the economy. Three months later, the king replaced his half-brother as crown prince—a former intelligence chief who'd been appointed deputy crown prince by King Abdullah just two years earlier—and placed his nephew and son in the line of succession. The king's decree said the move had been approved by a majority of the Al Saud family's Allegiance Council. Prince Mohammed was given control over Saudi Aramco by royal decree 48 hours later.

The prince divides his time between his father's palaces and the Defense Ministry, working from morning until after midnight most days. Courtiers claim his relationship with the crown prince, Mohammed bin Nayef, is good; they have neighboring camps at the royals' desert encampment. Prince Mohammed takes frequent meetings with the king and spends long sessions with consultants and aides poring over economic and oil data. He also greets foreign dignitaries and diplomats and is the main prosecutor of Saudi Arabia's controversial war in Yemen against Iran-backed Houthi rebels. For all the prince's talk of thrift, the war has cost a fortune. "We believe that we are closer than ever to a political solution," he says about the conflict. "But if things relapse, we are ready."

He's awakened most mornings by his kids, two boys and two girls, ranging in age from 1 to 6. That's the last he sees of them. "Sometimes my wife gets upset with me because I put so much pressure on her for the programs that I want them to have," he says. "I rely mainly on their mother for their upbringing." Prince Mohammed has only one wife and isn't planning on marrying more, he says. His generation isn't so into polygamy, he explains. Life is too busy, compared with past eras when farmers could work a few hours a day and warriors could "take spoils once a week and had a lot of spare time." Working, sleeping, eating, and drinking don't leave a lot of time to open another household, he says. "It's tough [enough] living with one family."

In Prince Mohammed, the U.S. may find a sympathetic long-term ally in a chaotic region. After President Obama met the prince at Camp David last May, he said he found him "extremely knowledgeable, very smart, and wise beyond his years." The prince visited Obama at the White House in September to air his disapproval of the U.S.-brokered nuclear deal with Iran, and the two men were likely to meet again on April 20 when Obama visits King Salman in Riyadh.

In March, Republican Senator Lindsey Graham of South Carolina met Prince Mohammed in Riyadh with a delegation from Congress. The prince emerged wearing his traditional gold-laced robe and red headdress and confided to Graham that he wished he'd worn something else. "He said, 'The robe does not make the man,'" Graham says. "He obviously understands our culture." Graham says the men spoke for an hour about the "common enemies" that Israel and Saudi Arabia have in Islamic State and Iran; innovation and Islam; and, of course, the epic economic changes. "I was blown away; I couldn't get over how comfortable meeting him was," says Graham. "What you have is a guy who sees the finite nature of the revenue stream and, rather than panicking, sees a strategic opportunity. His view of Saudi society is that basically it's now time to have less for the few and more for the many. The top members of the royal family have been identified by their privilege. He wants them to be identified by their obligations instead."

Changing the royal optics in a country where thousands of Al Sauds live opulently off the national coffers won't be easy, but Prince Mohammed is willing to try. "The opportunities we have," he says, "are much bigger than the problems."

—*With Glen Carey, Deema Almashabi, Vivian Nereim, Wael Mahdi, Javier Blas, Alaa Shahine, Riad Hamade, Matthew Philips, and Zainab Fattah*

(Update: Clarifies a description of the relationship between Saudi Arabia and Israel.)

Appendix D
How Did We Get Here?

This is the original research conducted by Victoria Gurevich in response to questions posed by the author. Portions of the book were extracted from this research, but I wanted to give the reader the benefit of her extensive effort.

Victoria Gurevich is a freelance researcher and writer based in New York. Her work explores geopolitical events and conflicts and their historic and contemporary ramifications.

March 3, 2016

Question: What were the national/natural boundaries of the Middle East prior to World War I, and what were their economies based on? What was the relative strength of their economies—to each other and to the world?

Answer: World War I was a pivotal moment in history: the eight-hundred-year-old Ottoman Empire, which spanned from the Bosporus Strait through Mesopotamia[1] and into the Persian Gulf, was dismantled. Existing as one empire at the time, the area of the Ottoman Empire occupied present-day Turkey, Iraq, Syria, Lebanon, Israel, Palestine, Jordan, Saudi Arabia, and the Hijaz. The territory of the Ottoman Empire was quickly reclaimed by other world powers, creating much of the national landscape of the Middle East today. Before World War I, the Middle East was occupied by the Ottoman Empire, Persia, the tribes of the Arabian Peninsula, and many other Bedouin groups. The borders of any regional powers' jurisdiction were approximate and not as systematically divided as European territory was at the time. The majority of Middle Eastern inhabitants led seminomadic lifestyles. Existing industry was concentrated in urban centers, operated by the elite, wealthy merchant class, and produced goods predominantly for export. Both the seminomadic tribes and the urban merchant class were vital to the social, cultural, and economic makeup of their nations. The economies of both the Ottoman Empire and Persia at the dawn of the twentieth century were in decline, and the Arabian Peninsula was not yet united under a single government, leaving various tribes of the region to operate their economies independently.

Historical Context

Compared to the meticulously cartographed region we know today, the Middle East prior to World War I was loosely bound by national boundaries and administered approximately by tribal rulers. Prior to its dissolution and partition, the Ottoman Empire stretched from the Bosporus Strait down through what is present-day Iraq and connected to the Persian Gulf, and the division of this vast empire guided the delineation of national boundaries in the region. In addition to Ottoman influence,

Persia and the Saudi Kingdom were also regional powers that were considered (although not consulted) in the partitioning and coronating of the Middle East. It is important to note that while boundaries have been drawn around the various countries and territories, they signify the approximate control that any capital assumed to possess. Even well within these approximate borders, Bedouin tribes often ruled regional territories, limiting a capital's influence. Especially after the revolution in Tehran in 1906 that ended the shah's regime, "the political system proved unstable, and its authority was very weak outside the capital."[2]

The seminomadic nature of the majority of Middle Eastern inhabitants at the dawn of the twentieth century influenced the economies that supported their existence, as "70–80 percent [of people living in the Middle East] lived outside the large towns and made their living either from cultivation, or herding, or a combination of the two."[3] Industry did exist, although in much smaller proportions and in more heavily populated areas, and it often produced goods for export such as "sugar, cigarettes, carpets, and silk thread"[4] for European markets. To consider the economies of the region prior to World War I more closely, I will briefly elaborate on the economic activities of Persia, the region of Arabia, and the Ottoman Empire.

As mentioned earlier, the territory of Persia was not closely administered, and national economic activities were concentrated around the capital of Tehran. A comprehensive census does not exist for this time; however, in 1815, John Marshall estimated that approximately six million people lived in Persia, half leading nomadic lifestyles.[5] An assessment of the Persian economy during the Qajar dynasty, which ruled from 1789 to 1925, suggests the following: "In terms of the basic economic structure, Persia depicted the key features of a backward economy: the predominance of land-related and agricultural activities in the nation's livelihood; primitive and limited road and infrastructure networks; a low degree of urbanization, despite a somewhat favorable rate compared with pre-industrial Europe; and limited, although increasing, internal and external trade."[6] Toward the end of the dynasty, the kingdom also suffered from a depreciating currency, rising prices, and a growing fiscal crisis, so that by 1914, "the Persian currency was only one-fifth of what it had been worth in 1800."[7] Many factors contributed to the financial and political decline of Persia. Shaul Bakhash notes that "the fiscal crisis was brought about by an inadequate, ineffective, and inefficient fiscal administration; astronomical costs of maintaining state bureaucracies, the army, and the royal court; and outright corruption and decay deeply rooted in both the central and provincial governments and their various departments."[8] Oil exploration did not begin in Persia until 1901, when a private citizen, William D'Arcy, purchased petroleum exploration rights from Persia. D'Arcy did not seek out this endeavor but was approached by a Persian emissary who was selling petroleum concessions in Persia in order to support the kingdom's crippling finances. When oil was struck in 1908, the original concession in 1901 between D'Arcy and the Shah granted Persia only 16 percent of the net profits.[9] By 1914, oil in Persia made up less than 1 percent of total world output.

The Ottoman Empire claimed suzerainty[10] over most of the Arabian Peninsula, which was ruled by a patchwork of tribal kingdoms until 1932, when the modern state of Saudi Arabia was established. Before World War I, there were four major centers of activity; however, because of the harsh terrain of the peninsula, the kingdoms of Nejd, Hijaz, Al Hasa, and Asir operated independently of one another and with infrequent confrontation (unless a conquest was undertaken). Hijaz was the most profitable of the four regions thanks to the presence of the cities of Mecca and Medina, holy Islamic sites that attracted thousands of pilgrims annually. The pilgrimage to the region and subsequent trade not only sustained the Hijaz economy but also guided the economy of Saudi Arabia until the discovery of oil in 1938. The income from the holy sites affected only a small few; thus the economic activities sustaining the livelihoods of the rest of the Arabian population were predominantly agrarian-based.

Spanning from Budapest to the Persian Gulf and from Algiers to the Caspian Sea, the Ottoman Empire connected the East to the West, and its capital city of Istanbul was the crossroads. However, despite Istanbul being a major trade location, the rest of the empire was engaged in predominantly agrarian activities. It is challenging to compare the strength of the economies of the aforementioned territories because their social, political, and economic organizations are strikingly different.

Question: What were the national boundaries after the Sykes-Picot Treaty?

Answer: Mesopotamia, a former territory of the Ottoman Empire, was the subject of the Sykes-Picot Agreement, which partitioned the area thought to be rich in oil reserves. France controlled the area encompassing modern-day Syria, Lebanon, northern Iraq, and southeastern Turkey, while the British controlled what is now Jordan, southern Iraq, and southern Palestine. The area from Jerusalem to Haifa was to be internationally administered but came under British mandate in 1922 after a decision from the League of Nations. Within the spheres of influence that Britain and France were granted, the level of direct or indirect control was up to their discretion.

Historical Context

When oil was discovered in Persia in 1908, the oil enterprise was quickly expanded from one drill site to several more; however, while activities increased in Persia, all eyes were on Mesopotamia, "an area thought to be highly prospective in oil."[11] As World War I progressed, the British and French, in a 1915 agreement known as the Sykes-Picot, preemptively partitioned the region of Mesopotamia in anticipation of the dissolution of the Ottoman Empire. For both Britain and France, the ownership and security of reliable oil reserves was a war aim, leading to disagreement over the delineation of borders that guarded their objectives. It wasn't until 1920, at a meeting of the Allied Supreme Council, that an agreement over borders was reached. Known as the San Remo Agreement, Mesopotamia was divided as follows:

> Two "A" mandates were created out of the old Ottoman province of Syria: the northern half (Syria and Lebanon) was mandated to France, the southern half (Palestine) to Great Britain. The province of Mesopotamia (Iraq) was also mandated to Great Britain. Under the terms of an "A" mandate the individual countries were deemed independent but subject to a mandatory power until they reached political maturity. . . . An Anglo-French oil agreement was also

concluded . . . providing France with a 25 percent share of Iraqi oil and favorable oil transport terms and stipulating in return the inclusion of Mosul in the British mandate of Iraq.[12]

Question: What part did the British play in switching their fleet from coal to oil?

Answer: In order to advance the naval race that was underway between Britain and Germany, the Royal Navy, in 1912, commissioned entire fleets of ships to be built—ships that were powered by oil instead of coal. The commitment to oil as a primary fuel source was made before a reliable source of petroleum was secured. Once this entire industry was dependent on oil, a race to find reserves began. Oil extraction was already underway in Persia, but attention was turned toward Mesopotamia. British ambitions for the region were guided by the need to secure a reliable petroleum source for the Royal Navy. The Sykes-Picot Agreement was the means by which Britain was able to establish a claim over the oil-rich territory.

Historical Context

Before oil was discovered in the Middle East, the Shell Transport and Trading Company (a Dutch and British enterprise) first struck oil in Borneo in 1897. But "the chemical characteristics of the Borneo crude were such as to yield little kerosene. It could, however, be used, unrefined as a fuel oil," which was not valued in Britain at the turn of the century.[13] Russia had been using the waste residue from kerosene to operate its ships on the Caspian Sea since the 1870s, demonstrating the substance's high capacity and efficiency. In Britain and most of Western Europe, however, the role of oil as fuel was still minor. The only industry that occasionally used oil was the railway industry when it needed to reduce smog in major cities or when "carrying members of the royal family."[14] Because coal supported industrial development, all of the major industries rebuffed the vision of oil as a primary source of fuel, and none more aggressively than the Royal Navy.

That was in 1897, when the Royal Navy was under the command of a first sea lord who was more comfortable relying on Welsh coal than on a distant and untested source of fuel. In 1904, however, an oil enthusiast, John Arbuthnot Fisher, rose to the rank of first sea lord, and he believed that "oil fuel . . . will absolutely revolutionize naval strategy."[15] Strategically, "Oil offered many benefits. It had double the thermal content of coal so that boilers could be smaller and ships could travel twice as far. Greater speed was possible and oil burned with less smoke so the fleet would not reveal its presence as quickly. Oil could be stored in tanks anywhere, allowing more efficient design of ships, and it could be transferred through pipes without reliance on stokers, reducing manning. Refueling at sea was feasible, which provided greater flexibility."[16]

Despite Fisher's personal views about the merits of oil, the majority of the Royal Navy met him with resistance. The oil question may have sat unresolved for several years, if not decades, had it not been for the growing presence of Germany. Because it was the Royal Navy that solidified Britain's status as a world power, that was the industry that Germany sought to overtake. The impetus for advancement stemmed from the naval race between Britain and Germany, with the latter competing for prominence and the former maneuvering so as not to have to share the world stage. By 1911, "the Navy had already built or was building 56 destroyers solely dependent on oil and 74 submarines that could only be driven by oil"; however, the most important part of the fleet, the battleships, were still powered by coal.[17] When Winston Churchill joined the Navy as first lord of the Admiralty, the highest position any civilian could hold in the Royal Navy, he undertook a series of programs in 1912, 1913, and 1914 that introduced entire fleets of ships fed only by oil, "on which our life depended."[18]

Churchill's decision to convert to oil raised a serious problem, however, in that the switch was made before a reliable supply of oil has been secured. At the time, two viable oil companies existed with which the Admiralty could establish a partnership: Royal Dutch/Shell in Borneo and Anglo-Persian in Persia. While Shell was more established, the Admiralty and its associates, "all patriotic Englishmen, were willing to sacrifice the economic advantage that would accrue from affiliating with Shell and instead keep the company independent."[19] Eleven days after Parliament approved Churchill's bill to purchase 51 percent of Anglo-Persian and sign onto a twenty-year contract for fuel oil, World War I had begun. From 1912 to 1918, oil production in Persia "grew more than tenfold," while still only accounting for 1 percent of total world output by 1914. Toward the middle of the war, "oil potential in Mesopotamia was beginning to loom larger in British military and political planning," and the Sykes-Picot Agreement secured, not only for Britain, but also for the Royal Navy, strategic assets.[20]

Question: What was the role of oil and the new political boundaries in creating the governments that eventually rose to power? What friction ensued as a result of the new boundaries? How did oil affect the political situation in the Middle East? Did Sykes-Picot create an immediate Arab resistance movement, or did it develop over time?

Answer: After dividing the Levant along straight lines and without respect for the ethnic, cultural, or religious differences of the inhabitants, the Sykes-Picot Agreement served as the basis for the founding of Syria, Jordan, Iraq, Lebanon, and Palestine. Britain and France were granted mandates over their respective territories, which they could administer as desired. Britain appointed governments in Iraq and Jordan, while France appointed the government of Syria and Lebanon. Palestine remained as a British protectorate until 1948. Oil was the main motivator for investing in the region; however, other than in Iraq, oil does not account for a significant portion of state revenue for the countries that emerged as a result of Sykes-Picot. Before the Sykes-Picot Agreement was reached, the Levant was part of the Ottoman Empire and was populated by people of different ethnicities, religions, and sects. The neat lines that were drawn by British and French mandates acknowledged the matrix of the region, but did not anticipate how integral it was to maintaining amicability between peoples. The grievances that were felt after the creation of state boundaries differed between each state and developed at different times; however, the majority of the problems that plague the region today can be traced back to the 1916 partition.

Historical Context

During World War I, the sharif of Mecca was encouraged to lead an "Arab revolt against Turkey," in return for which he and his sons were promised to be installed as rulers of the new states of the Levant. Britain put Faisal, the third son of Hussein

Sharif of Mecca, on the throne of Syria; however, Faisal was deposed once control passed to France.[21] Not wanting to waste the talent or allegiance of Faisal, Britain recommissioned him as the monarch of constitutional Iraq. The territory of Iraq in 1921 comprised diverse groups including "Shia Arabs and Sunni Arabs, Jews and Kurds and Yazidis" and was a "territory with few important cities, most of the countryside under the control of local sheikhs, and with little common political or cultural history, but with a rising Arab nationalism."[22] Into this arrangement, Britain wished to introduce constitutionalism and parliament. Vestigial of the Ottoman Empire, the Sunni Arabs continued to hold political power, despite the Shia being by far the most numerous. Until the British mandate of Iraq was terminated in 1932, British forces played a central and effective role in suppressing Shia and Kurdish rebellions for independence. Once British forces left, however, Iraq experienced a series of rebellions and coups that have left the country in a chronic state of instability. British manipulation of the region spurred the Arab nationalist movements that would resurface in the country and region for decades to come.

While British mandate also existed over the territory of Jordan, the history of this protectorate has proven to be more stable. Abdullah, another son of Hussein, assumed the throne as the amirate of Transjordan in 1921.[23] Abdullah had a significantly easier task than his brother Faisal in that the population of Jordan was much less varied than that of Iraq. As a result, there was less ethnic and sectarian tension. Abdullah stayed in power as emir until 1946, when the British mandate ended, and then remained as king of independent Jordan until his assassination in 1951.[24] Oil had little influence in the formation or economic prosperity of Jordan, as the area has no petroleum deposits and relies on imports for all of its energy needs. To this day, Jordan remains one of the most stable nations in the Middle East and has managed to avoid the resistance movements that have taken root in other parts of the region. It is important to note that Britain and France chose to manage their mandates very differently. The Middle East Policy Council sets forth the following: "Britain's interest in the provinces focused on safeguarding the route to India, securing cheap and accessible oil for the Empire's needs, maintaining the balance of power in the Mediterranean to its advantage, and protecting its financial concerns. France hoped to preserve her centuries-old ties with the Syrian Catholics, gain a strategic and economic base in the eastern Mediterranean, ensure a cheap supply of cotton and silk and prevent Arab nationalism from infecting her North African empire."[25]

Once the French were formally granted their mandate over Syria in 1920, they assumed control over six distinct provinces, Lebanon being one of them; the French introduced "new national identities, citizenship and social class," all of which challenged and even replaced "the identities of clan, tribe and religion."[26] A territory at first, Lebanon was inaugurated as independent from Syria because of the large, although still minority, population of Maronite Christians whom the French regarded favorably. The borders of Lebanon were constructed thoughtfully so as to not include too many Muslim communities, which would threaten the Maronites' position of power. The new country of Lebanon, formed in 1941, was not influenced by the oil industry, as there were no petroleum deposits in the area. Resistance to divisions introduced as a result of Sykes-Picot did not boil over until 1975, when the Lebanese Civil War erupted. The war was fought over the political influence that the

Maronites held amid a growing Muslim population, and the conflict's end result was that the national Muslim majority assumed political power.

While Lebanon was removed from the Greater Syrian mandate, the remaining conglomerate of ethnicities and religious sects was amalgamated in Syria. Pan-Arab nationalistic sentiments were felt early on in Syria, although the French went to great lengths to suppress these sentiments. From 1920 (when the San Remo Agreement was officially issued) until 1945 (when the mandate was over), Greater Syria existed under multiple forms of government that kept Arab political unity at bay. Different administrations governed the numerous ethnic and religious groups that resided in Syria, often reorganizing every couple of years.[27] After Syria was granted independence in 1946, the country suffered numerous military coups and revolts for the next several decades, driven by feelings of disenfranchisement and nationalist sentiments. Oil was discovered in Syria in 1956 but did not develop into a reliable industry until over a decade later. Oil's late introduction into the Syrian economy was not a factor that influenced the political situation of its early history. The oil reserves in the country are not of a marketable quantity, although they do account for a significant portion of economic revenues.

Question: When Standard Oil went to Saudi Arabia, what were the immediate effects in the region? What was the impact of the formation of Saudi Aramco?

Answer: After uniting the tribes on the Arabian Peninsula in 1930, Ibn Saud's kingdom was running out of money. In 1933, to raise revenue for the state, Ibn Saud granted Standard Oil (SoCal) a concession to search for oil. When oil was found in 1938, Ibn Saud expanded the area in which SoCal could drill to just over 50 percent of Saudi Arabia. Ibn Saud spent the money from oil revenues lavishly on personal expenses, with little benefit reaching the rest of Saudi citizens. It wasn't until the rule of King Faisal in the 1960s that modernization reforms were undertaken. The nationalization of Saudi Aramco, transferred from US ownership, was a gradual process that was completed in 1980 (the name was changed from Aramco to Saudi Aramco in 1988). Saudi Aramco became the largest state-held supply of oil reserves and accounted for over 65 percent of state revenue in 1980. The nationalization of Aramco solidified the rentier state that had been developing in Saudi Arabia since the 1940s.[28]

Historical Context

Shortly after the end of World War I, the US was faced with the threat of exhausting its domestic oil reserves within several decades. While discussion about the prospect of shale oil in the mountains of Colorado, Utah, and Nevada was ongoing, the US oil industries and American government turned their search for oil outward. Invoking the "Open Door" policy, the United States called for equal access for American businesses in the Middle East, particularly Mesopotamia. When news of the San Remo Agreement of 1920 reached the United States, it was denounced as "old fashioned imperialism" and "seemed to violate the principle of equal rights among the victorious Allies."[29] Diplomatic dialogue between the United States, Britain, and France resulted in an agreement that that it was in the best interests of all parties that American companies be allowed to develop the region. However, the Middle East could not be opened for just one company; Jersey Standard outranked all the other players in size and scope. Access to the Middle East was granted to a consortium of American companies whose interests were held by the Near East Development Company.

A contract was signed between Royal Dutch/Shell, Anglo-Persian, the French, and the Near East Development Company, granting each signatory 23.75 percent of the oil, and 5 percent for Calouste Gulbenkian, an Armenian businessman who was an investor in the Turkish Petroleum Company (TPC).[30] The participants were also bound by a "self-denying" clause (also known as the Red Line Agreement), which stipulated that no company was able to develop oil fields without the support of the other members. There was, however, a loophole in this agreement. While the self-denying clause prohibited any signatory company of Turkish Petroleum from seeking private concessions, it did not prohibit nonmember companies from doing so.

In the late 1920s, Bahrain had been attempting to sell oil concessions; however, a geological report conducted in Saudi Arabia in 1926 stated that the prospects of oil on the peninsula left "little room for optimism," and no member of the TPC was willing to risk investing in the region.[31] Standard Oil of California (SoCal), however, which was not a signatory of the Red Line Agreement, wanted to secure oil resources outside of the United States and won the Bahrain oil concession in 1930. SoCal set up a subsidiary company, the Bahrain Petroleum Company, and struck oil in Bahrain in 1932. Situated only twenty miles away from the mainland and with geology similar to Saudi Arabia's, Bahrain's oil reserves seemingly contradicted the report that had deterred potential prospectors for half of a decade. To continue their exploration, SoCal turned to Saudi Arabia.

Abdul Aziz—later known as Ibn Saud—spent the first three decades of the twentieth century conquering Arabia to fulfill his dream of reestablishing the Saudi dynasty. In 1930, Ibn Saud had accomplished his mission of uniting the Arabian Peninsula and commemorated the feat by renaming the realm from "the Kingdom of the Hejaz and Nejd and Its Dependencies" to its current moniker: Saudi Arabia. In 1932, however, the new kingdom was quickly running out of money as a result of the onset of the Great Depression, which significantly reduced the number of pilgrims traveling to the holy sites. Ibn Saud did not wish to see his country transformed into an oil state, because of the risk that "foreign capital and technicians could disturb, perhaps even disrupt, traditional values and relationships." However, selling an oil concession to search for oil, with no guarantee that any oil was to be found, was a small gamble.[32] SoCal won the concessions and agreed to pay the king a £30,000 interest-free loan, another £25,000 loan 18 months later, and £5,000 annually. The SoCal oil concession that was administered by the California Arabian standard Oil Company (Casoc) subsidiary—renamed the Arabian American Oil Company (Aramco) in 1944 after joining with Texas Oil—was the only exclusively American-owned and -operated petroleum venture in the Middle East.[33]

Oil was struck in 1938, and after Aramco received a royalties check for $1.5 million, the concession was expanded to over 50 percent of Saudi Arabia. Aramco went from producing 11,000 barrels a day in 1939 to more than 477,000 barrels a decade later, "accounting for slightly more than 5 percent of total world production and 35 percent of all Middle East production."[34] The wealth from the new oil industry was not used to elevate society; rather, Ibn Saud spent his royalties on personal extravagance and political favors. It wasn't until the mid-1960s, under the reign of King Faisal, that reforms and modernization were undertaken in Saudi Arabia.

A report in 1949 revealed that Aramco was paying more to the United States in taxes than it was paying to Saudi Arabia in royalties, a division that was unacceptable to Saudi Arabia.[35] That same year, Saudi Arabia took up negotiations to establish a profit-sharing arrangement, which was reached in 1951 at a fifty-fifty agreement with Aramco. For the next twenty-five years, the arrangement stayed in place; however, thoughts of nationalization brewed below the surface. In 1970, Saudi Aramco—the national company that would eventually take over the foreign-owned Aramco—was formed. Unlike other nationalizations, the handover of Aramco was done gradually, with the king taking over in 1980 and the name of the company being officially changed in 1988. The two countries—the United States and Saudi Arabia—maintained close business relations, with the latter being the owner and the former being the operator. Aramco (the American companies) would continue to market Saudi oil and receive "twenty-one cents a barrel."[36] The nationalization of Saudi Aramco strengthened the rentier economy that already characterized Saudi Arabia. By 1979, "the oil sector accounted for 65% of economic activity" with investments being driven by the state. As such, Saudi citizens enjoyed "heavily subsidized public utilities, state employment, free education and healthcare," all without paying taxes.[37] The nationalization of Saudi Aramco, in addition to changing the social lives of citizens, also affected political life. By not collecting taxes, the Saudi government was not responsible to its citizens, and political participation and criticism were slowly eradicated.

Question: How much of a role did oil play in enhancing the economies/quality of life in the Middle East? What is the relative strength of their economies today? A short country-by-country history/analysis of the effects of the Sykes-Picot Treaty and oil would be helpful.

Answer: The role of oil in enhancing the economies and quality of life varied from state to state and over time. Except for Iraq, the role of oil in the countries created as a result of Sykes-Picot was minor if not nonexistent. Instead of oil being found in large quantities in Mesopotamia, as was predicted in the early twentieth century, the Arabian Peninsula, a region not covered by Sykes-Picot, was where oil was found in marketable quantities.

Iran—Persia, not involved in the Sykes-Picot Agreement, changed its name to Iran in the 1930s. A rentier state, Iran has been dependent on oil revenues since it was first discovered in 1908. Beginning in 1925, Mohammed Reza Shah began modernizing Iran economically, socially, and culturally. Modernization elevated some but left many groups behind, especially the more traditional and rural demographics. While the quality of life has increased in the aggregate, a greater division has been created between the wealthy and the poor. Additionally, while state-owned oil revenues have fueled growth, they have also eliminated government accountability and quelled political participation. Rentier economies, while wealthy, are also vulnerable as a result of the volatility of the market.

Iranian economist Hossein Mahdavy introduced the rentier state concept in 1970 and others, notably Giacomo Luciani, elaborated and applied it to the emerging Arab Gulf States. Applying the notion of a rentier state implied that democratization in the region was iffy at best. This analysis is based on the observation that the vast amounts raised by oil-rich governments have little to do with taxation, being instead unearned revenue from the extraction of a natural resource. So long as states have sufficient amounts of such income, rentier state theory suggests that they may have little reason to democratize, reform, or otherwise evolve.[38]

Because the state relies on revenues from the sale of natural resources for the majority of its GDP, other sectors of society remain underdeveloped. Nevertheless, the economy of Iran is the second largest in the Middle East and North Africa.

Iraq—As discussed previously, Sykes-Picot granted the British a mandate over Iraq, which was chosen because of its oil reserves. The ethnic and religious composition of Iraq at the time of the formation of the state was varied, with political power being concentrated in the minority group. Likewise, the revenues from the sale of oil in the rentier economy were concentrated among the minority Sunni population. Oil revenues in Iraq's rentier economy also were concentrated in this minority group. Iraq had a tumultuous start after the British mandate ended in 1932, making economic development difficult and gradual as the country endured numerous coups and revolutions. Today, the economy and government of Iraq are threatened by the expansion of ISIL in the Levant.

Saudi Arabia—Saudi Arabia, not affected by the Sykes-Picot Agreement, has the largest economy in the Middle East and North Africa. Saudi Arabia is the definition of a rentier economy and therefore secures significant state revenues from a single industry, leaving the rest of the economy vulnerable to market fluctuations. Oil revenues in Saudi Arabia are very much responsible for the quality of life the country can afford (although modernization reforms were not undertaken until the 1960s, several decades after wealth from oil revenues was reliably had). The exchange for material wealth is the implicit social contract that buys consent.

Lebanon, Syria, Jordan, Palestine—For the other countries that emerged as a result of Sykes-Picot, oil has played a minor role in the development of their economies and society. There are no oil reserves in Lebanon, Jordan, and Palestine, and oil was not discovered in Syria until 1956. While Syria is not a major oil producer by Middle East standards, oil revenues do make up a significant portion of the Syrian economy. The close relationship between Syria and Russia today was established in 1946, when the Soviet Union and the fledgling state of Syria "signed a secret agreement stating that the new nation of Syria would provide diplomatic and political support to the USSR in exchange for military aid and assistance in forming a national army."[39] Syria then became a client state of the Soviet Union during the Cold War and adopted a socialist economic model, closing its economy. The imposition of sanctions by the United States during the Cold War years limited the economy further, as did another wave of sanctions in the mid-2000s. The economies of Jordan and Lebanon are emerging markets that have seen promising growth rates in the past decade or so but that will be tested by the ongoing regional crisis.

Bahrain—The first oil discovery on the Arab side of the Gulf was made in Bahrain; however, the supply was small by Middle East standards. Bahrain has diversified its economy so that oil revenues account for a small portion of GDP, while the banking sector has become an active industry. Thanks to Bahrain's small population, quality of life in the country has been ranked highly, consequently attracting a significant number of non-national employees. Society in Bahrain represents a mix of nationalities and religions.

Kuwait—After threats from the Ottoman Empire, Kuwait became a British protectorate in 1899. In exchange for naval protection, Kuwait allowed Britain to control its foreign affairs.[40] When oil was discovered in Kuwait in 1937, revenues were used to modernize its commercial center and raise the standard of living to the high quality enjoyed today. Kuwait is heavily dependent on oil, with revenues from the industry accounting for 90 percent of the national budget.[41] Unlike in other rentier states, Kuwait in recent years has seen increasing political participation and social modernization.

In the late 1960s, when Britain decided to withdraw from the Persian Gulf, the United States was faced with a strategic dilemma regarding influence in the region. For the first half of the twentieth century, Britain's role in the Middle East had been that of a protector, guaranteeing that trade routes and oil sources went undisturbed. After World War I, however, Britain was faced with "deepening British financial weakness, bruising domestic political debate over the priorities and values of British foreign policy, and increasingly intractable and violent nationalist sentiment in the Middle East.[42]" Britain announced in 1968 that it was withdrawing its military presence from the Middle East, meaning that without the naval fleet it could no longer safeguard global oil interests in the region, a resource that was essential for the developed world. Threatened with Cold War tensions and given the potential power vacuum in the region, the US wanted to establish a defense against Soviet infiltration into the Middle East. Not wanting to become entangled in the region directly but still exert influence, Nixon's decision, dubbed the "Twin Pillars Strategy," was to establish Iran and Saudi Arabia as regional powers, surrogates that would act in accordance with US interests. The "pillars" were encouraged to acquire copious amounts of advanced arms from the US government to support their new roles as "regional policemen."

Succeeding Nixon, President Jimmy Carter declared in his State of the Union address, "Let our position be absolutely clear: An attempt by any outside force to gain control of the Persian Gulf region will be regarded as an assault on the vital interests of the United States of America, and such an assault will be repelled by any means necessary, including military force."[43] While the Twin Pillars Strategy initially was meant to equip regional powers to protect their own resources, thereby making unnecessary any direct US involvement, the strategy instead ushered in a pattern of militarism that contributed to the destabilization of the region. In a piece titled *America, Oil, and War in the Middle East*, Toby Craig Jones offers the following:

The pattern of militarism that began in the Persian Gulf in the 1970s has partly been the product of American support for and deliberate militarization of brutal *and* vulnerable authoritarian regimes. Massive weapons sales to oil autocrats and the decision to build a geopolitical military order in the Gulf that depended on and empowered those rulers resulted in a highly militarized and fragile balance of power. And from the 1970s on, oil-producing states have faced repeated internal and external threats, including domestic unrest, invasion, and regional or civil war, or at least the imminent prospect of turmoil. Such instability and conflict has had much to do, of course, with internal political problems, only some of which were the result of outside intervention. But the militarization that began in earnest under the United States' watch exacerbated and accelerated those uncertainties and helped further destabilize oil-producing states and the region.[44]

With the Iranian Revolution of 1979, the Twin Pillars Strategy was no longer supported, but the transactional relationship, oil for guns, continued. In response to the Iran-Iraq war that broke out in 1980, the other pillar, Saudi Arabia, along with five other Persian Gulf states—Kuwait, Oman, Bahrain, Qatar, and UAE—formed the Gulf Cooperation Council (GCC) in 1981. United by their economic similarities and political structures, the GCC facilitates cooperation between the energy-rich Gulf states. In addition to economic partnerships, the GCC also serves as a military coalition.

Notes

1. Mesopotamia was the region along the Tigris and Euphrates rivers and referred to the area of what is present-day Iraq, northern Syria, and some parts of Kurdistan. The region of Mesopotamia, which existed under the Ottoman Empire, was renamed after 1918 when the Sykes-Picot Treaty delineated the borders of the region.

2. Daniel Yergin, *The Prize: The Epic Quest for Oil, Money and Power* (New York: Touchstone, 1991), 145.

3. Roger Owen and Sevket Pamuk, *A History of Middle East Economies in the Twentieth Century* (London: I.B. Tauris Publishers, 1998), 3.

4. Ibid., 4.

5. Hassan Hakimian, "Economy viii. In the Qajar Period," in *Encyclopedia Iranica*, December 15, 1997, http://www.iranicaonline.org/articles/economy-viii-in-the-qajar-period.

6. Ibid.

7. Ibid.

8. Hakimian, "Economy viii.

9. Mohammad Malek, "History of Iran: Oil in Iran between the Two World Wars," Iran Chamber Society, accessed February 19, 2016, http://www.iranchamber.com/history/articles/oil_iran_between_world_wars.php.

10. "Suzerainty" describes the relationship of a powerful state having control over the international relations and foreign policy of a vassal state. The state or region that is under the influence of the dominant entity is allowed limited self-rule in domestic affairs.

11. Yergin, *The Prize*, 184.

12. *Encyclopedia Britannica*, s.v., "Conference of San Remo," 2014, http://www.britannica.com/event/Conference-of-San-Remo.

13. Yergin, *The Prize*, 116.

14. Ibid.

15. Ibid., 151.

16. Erik Dahl, "Naval Innovation: From Coal to Oil," *Joint Force Quarterly*, Winter 2000–1, 50–56, http://www.dtic.mil/dtic/tr/fulltext/u2/a524799.pdf.

17. Yergin, *The Prize*, 155.

18. Ibid., 156.

19. Ibid., 158.

20. Ibid., 173.

21. Ibid., 200.

22. Ibid.

23. Ibid., 200.

24. Kamal Salibi, *The Modern History of Jordan* (New York: I.B. Tauris, 1999).

25. Ayse Tekdal Fildis, "The Troubles in Syria: Spawned by French Divide and Rule," *The Middle East Policy Council* 18, no. 4 (2011), http://www.mepc.org/journal/middle-east -policy-archives/troubles-syria-spawned-french-divide-and-rule.

26. Ibid.

27. Fildis, "Troubles in Syria."

28. A rentier state is one in which the state secures tremendous amounts of revenue from the sale of a natural resource, often oil. Because the high revenues come from the sale of natural resources and not taxation, citizens of rentier states are able to enjoy high standards of living but have limited opportunities for political participation. Rentier states are not accountable to their citizens in the ways that governments funded by taxation are. As a result, the exchange that is made between a rentier state and its citizens is material wealth for political consent.

29. Yergin, *The Prize*, 195.

30. Ibid., 204.

31. Ibid., 281.

32. Ibid., 284.

33. Rachel Bronson, *Thicker than Oil: America's Uneasy Partnership with Saudi Arabia* (Oxford: Oxford University Press, 2008), 18.

34. Ibid., 19.

35. Ann Genova and Toyin Falola, *The Politics of the Global Oil Industry: An Introduction* (Westport, CT: Praeger Publishers, 2005), 55.

36. Yergin, *The Prize*, 652.

37. Steffen Hertog, "A Rentier Social Contract: The Saudi Political Economy since 1979," Middle East Institute, last modified February 22, 2012, http://www.mei.edu/content/rentier -social-contract-saudi-political-economy-1979.

38. Riad Al Khouri, "Kuwait: Rentierism Revisited," Carnegie Endowment for International Peace, last modified September 9, 2008, http://carnegieendowment.org /sada/?fa=21948.

39. Kaeli Subberwal, "Echoes of the Cold War: Russia's Role in Syria," *The Gate*, last modified October 25, 2015, http://uchicagogate.com/2015/10/25/echoes-of-the-cold-war -russias-role-in-syria/.

40. BBC, "Kuwait Profile-Timeline," BBC Middle East, December 3, 2015, http://www.bbc .com/news/world-middle-east-14647211.

41. Reuters, "Oil Dependence Worries Kuwait," *Gulf News*, August 15, 2014, http:// gulfnews.com/business/sectors/markets/oil-dependence-worries-kuwait-1.851646.

42. Stephen McGlinchey, review of *American Ascendance, British Retreat, and the Rise of Iran in the Persian Gulf* by W. Taylor Fain, *E-International Relations*, November 15, 2010. https://www.e-ir.info/2010/11/15/american-ascendance-british-retreat-and-the-rise-of-iran -in-the-persian-gulf/.

43. Toby Craig Jones, "America, Oil, and War in the Middle East," *The Journal of American History* 99, no. 1 (2012): 208–18, doi:10.1093/jahist/jas045.

44. Ibid.

Selected Bibliography

The author has been careful to document the sources of quotes and others' thoughts throughout the book. There were other sources that generally helped to shape the logic and data of this book. Below is a list of selected sources that framed the author's work.

Ahmed, Irina, Josh Cohen, and Mihir Trivedi. "The Political Economy of Oil in the Middle East." Student Blog. Penn Wharton Public Policy Initiative, March 23, 2017. https://publicpolicy.wharton.upenn.edu/live/news/1778-the-political-economy-of-oil-in -the-middle-east.

Ballard, Gregory A. Changing the World: Indianapolis' Move to Post-Oil Vehicles. (white paper on energy security, City of Indianapolis, Indianapolis, December 12, 2012).

BBC. "Kuwait Profile-Timeline." BBC Middle East. December 3, 2015. http://www.bbc.com /news/world-middle-east-14647211.

Bronson, Rachel. Thicker Than Oil: America's Uneasy Partnership with Saudi Arabia. Oxford: Oxford University Press, 2008.

Central Intelligence Agency (CIA). World Factbook. Updated July 26, 2018. https://www.cia .gov/library/publications/the-world-factbook/.

Crawford, Neta C. "US spending on post 9/11 wars to reach 5.6 trillion by 2018." Providence, RI: Watson Institute for International and Public Affair, Brown University, 2017.

Dahl, Erik. "Naval Innovation: From Coal to Oil." Joint Force Quarterly, Winter 2000–01, 50–56. http://www.dtic.mil/dtic/tr/fulltext/u2/a524799.pdf.

Davis, Stacy C., Susan E. Williams, and Robert G. Boundy. Transportation Energy Data Book: Edition 36.1 (Oak Ridge, TN: Oak Ridge National Laboratory, April 2018), https://cta.ornl.gov/data/download36.shtml.

Davis, Stephen W. Center of Gravity and the War on Terrorism. Carlisle, PA: Strategy Research Project, US Army War College, 2003.

Encyclopedia Britannica. s.v. "Conference of San Remo." Accessed February 19, 2016. http:// www.britannica.com/event/Conference-of-San-Remo.

Fildis, Ayse Tekdal. "The Troubles in Syria: Spawned by French Divide and Rule." The Middle East Policy Council 18, no. 4 (2011). http://www.mepc.org/journal /middle-east-policy-archives/troubles-syria-spawned-french-divide-and-rule.

Genova, Ann, and Toyin Falola. The Politics of the Global Oil Industry: An Introduction. Westport, CT: Praeger, 2005.

Hakimian, Hassan. "Economy viii. In the Qajar Period." In Encyclopedia Iranica. December 15, 1997. http://www.iranicaonline.org/articles/economy-viii-in-the-qajar-period.

Hammel, Eric. The Root: The Marines in Beirut, August 1982–February 1984. St Paul, MN: Zenith, 2005.

Hertog, Steffan. "A Rentier Social Contract: The Saudi Political Economy since 1979." Middle East Institute. Last modified February 22, 2012. http://www.mei.edu/content /rentier-social-contract-saudi-political-economy-1979.

International Monetary Fund. "Economic Diversification in Oil-Exporting Arab

Countries." Paper prepared for the Annual Meeting of Arab Ministers of Finance, Manama, Bahrain, April 2016.

Jones, Toby Craig. "America, Oil, and War in the Middle East." *Journal of American History* 99, no. 1 (2012): 208–18. doi:10.1093/jahist/jas045.

Khouri, Riad Al. "Kuwait: Rentierism Revisited." Carnegie Endowment for International Peace. Last modified September 9, 2008. http://carnegieendowment.org/sada /?fa=21948.

Lugar Energy Initiative. Accessed August 1, 2018. Now available at https://www.webharvest .gov/congress112th/20121211213637/http://www.lugar.senate.gov/energy/.

Malek, Mohammad. "History of Iran: Oil in Iran between the Two World Wars." Iran Chamber Society. Accessed February 19, 2016. www.iranchamber.com/history/articles /oil_iran_between_world_wars.php.

Melosi, Martin. *The Automobile and the Environment in American History.* Accessed August 1, 2018. http://www.autolife.umd.umich.edu/.

McGlinchey, Stephen. "American Ascendance, British Retreat, and the rise of Iran in the Persian Gulf." E-International Relations. November 15, 2010. http://www.e-ir .info/2010/11/15/american-ascendance-british-retreat-and-the-rise-of-iran-in-the -persian-gulf/.

Owen, Roger, and Sevket Pamuk. *A History of Middle East Economies in the Twentieth Century.* London: I.B. Tauris, 1998.

Reilly, James. *A Strategic Level Center of Gravity Analysis on the Global War on Terrorism.* Carlisle, PA: Strategy Research Project, US Army War College, 2002.

Reuters. "Oil Dependence Worries Kuwait." *Gulf News,* August 15, 2011. http://gulfnews.com /business/sectors/markets/oil-dependence-worries-kuwait-1.851646.

Salibi, Kamal. *The Modern History of Jordan.* New York: I.B. Tauris, 1999.

Securing America's Future Energy (SAFE). Accessed August 1, 2018. https://secureenergy .org/.

Strange, Joe. *Centers of Gravity & Critical Vulnerabilities: Building on the Clausewitzian Foundation So That We Can All Speak the Same Language.* Quantico, VA: Marine Corps University, 1996.

Subberwal, Kaeli. "Echoes of the Cold War: Russia's Role in Syria." *The Gate.* Last modified October 25, 2015. http://uchicagogate.com/2015/10/25/echoes-of-the-cold-war-russias -role-in-syria/.

US Energy Information Administration (EIA) website. https://www.eia.gov/.

Yergin, Daniel. *The Prize: The Epic Quest for Oil, Money and Power.* New York: Touchtone, 1991.

After a twenty-three year career in the US Marine Corps and retiring as a Lieutenant Colonel, GREG BALLARD returned home to Indianapolis in 2001. In 2007, he ran a successful campaign to become the 48th Mayor of Indianapolis, subsequently serving two terms. While Mayor, he became a Trustee for the US Conference of Mayors and was known by his fellow mayors for his boldness and innovation. He holds a bachelor's degree in Economics from Indiana University, holds a Masters in Military Science, and was awarded Honorary Doctorates from Butler University and Marian University. He is currently a Visiting Fellow for Civic Leadership and Mayoral Archives at the University of Indianapolis. A Persian Gulf War veteran, he continues to be active in veteran causes as a member of the State of Indiana's Veterans' Affairs Commission and a board member of the Indiana War Memorials Foundation. His military decorations include the Legion of Merit, the Meritorious Service Medal with Gold Star, the Joint Service Commendation Medal, the Marine Corps Expeditionary Medal, and the Saudi and Kuwaiti Liberation of Kuwait Medals. Greg and his wife, Winnie, have been married for 35 years and have two children.